ENDANGERED

THEY SAW A
THYLACINE
Justine Campbell
and Sarah Hamilton

EXTINCTION
Hannie Rayson

THE
HONEY
BEES
Caleb Lewis

Currency Press,
Sydney

CURRENCY PLAYS

First published in 2017
by Currency Press Pty Ltd,
PO Box 2287, Strawberry Hills, NSW, 2012, Australia
enquiries@currency.com.au
www.currency.com.au

Copyright: *86 Billion—Plus Three—Reasons to Save the World* © Chris Mead, 2017; *They Saw a Thylacine* © Justine Campbell & Sarah Hamilton, 2013, 2017; *Extinction* © Hannie Rayson, 2012, 2017; *The Honey Bees* © Caleb Lewis, 2017.

COPYING FOR EDUCATIONAL PURPOSES

The Australian *Copyright Act 1968* (Act) allows a maximum of one chapter or 10% of this book, whichever is the greater, to be copied by any educational institution for its educational purposes provided that that educational institution (or the body that administers it) has given a remuneration notice to Copyright Agency Limited (CAL) under the Act. For details of the CAL licence for educational institutions contact CAL, 11/66 Goulburn Street, Sydney, NSW, 2000; tel: within Australia 1800 066 844 toll free; outside Australia 61 2 9394 7600; fax: 61 2 9394 7601; email: info@copyright.com.au

COPYING FOR OTHER PURPOSES

Except as permitted under the Act, for example a fair dealing for the purposes of study, research, criticism or review, no part of this book may be reproduced, stored in a retrieval system, or transmitted in any form or by any means without prior written permission. All enquiries should be made to the publisher at the address above.

Any performance or public reading of *They Saw a Thylacine*, *Extinction* or *The Honey Bees* is forbidden unless a licence has been received from the author or the author's agent. The purchase of this book in no way gives the purchaser the right to perform the plays in public, whether by means of a staged production or a reading. All applications for public performance should be addressed to the author/s c/- Currency Press.

Cataloguing-in-publication data for this title is available from the National Library of Australia website: www.nla.gov.au

Typeset by Dean Nottle for Currency Press.
Cover design by Studio Emma for Currency Press.

This project has been assisted by the Australian Government through the Australia Council, its arts funding and advisory body.

Contents

86 Billion—Plus Three—Reasons to Save the World v
  Chris Mead

THEY SAW A THYLACINE 1
  Justine Campbell & Sarah Hamilton

EXTINCTION 61
  Hannie Rayson

THE HONEY BEES 143
  Caleb Lewis

Currency Press acknowledges the Traditional Owners of the Country on which we live and work. We pay our respects to all Aboriginal and Torres Strait Islander Elders, past and present.

Katerina Kotsonis (left) as Kerrie and Rebecca Bower as Clover in Red Stitch Actors Theatre's 2016 production of THE HONEY BEES. (Photo: Jodie Hutchinson)

86 Billion—Plus Three—Reasons to Save the World

We are doing impossible things. The Mars Exploration Rovers, Cassini's amazing Enceladus fly-bys, the Kepler Space Mission—all defy incredible odds while looking for life, and we are doing it just for the greater good of human knowledge. That, and just in case humans might want to, might have to, desert the Earth for an alternate habitat. This, though, raises a fundamental question: why we don't just fix the pale blue dot we're already on?

To begin that undertaking however would suggest our culpability in the breaking of our planet in the first place, a responsibility these three plays all explore. This is an ethical, environmental, industrial, scientific and political mess—hence great drama—and one that sees us at a stalemate as the Doomsday Clock ticks ever closer to midnight.

For those of you too young to remember being haunted by the Doomsday Clock, let me scare you now: it was invented by a group who called themselves the Chicago Atomic Scientists in 1947 (most were Manhattan Project Alumnus) as a symbolic countdown to humanity's end/global catastrophe/nuclear cataclysm. It was seven minutes to midnight then; by the early '70s it was out past ten minutes to midnight; in 1991 with the ending of the Cold War it had relaxed to 17 minutes; in 2015 and 2016, however, it has accelerated back in, now at three minutes to midnight, the worst it has been since the US tested the H-bomb in 1953 (that first test revealing a weapon 450 times as powerful as the A-bomb that destroyed Nagasaki). The crucial thing to note about the Doomsday Clock is that what it's prophesying is entirely avoidable.

Before going any deeper into the slough of doom, AKA today's planet Earth, or remarking any further on our imminent and asymptomatic proximity to ecological devastation, I want to briefly discuss some extraordinary things—proton gradients and brain soup (and if I had more space, the secret life of trees)—that, like the plays, offer a spark, a shimmer, a flash of hope, or lines of flight towards actual, useful change.

It is appropriate, though, that a qualification is embedded here—why talk science in an introduction to three plays? My contention is that these plays bridge a gap that has emerged in the last 150 years: the artificial separation of science and art. Canadian novelist and biologist, Kristi Charish, asked in a 2012 speech to women in science and technology:

> Why is there such a disconnect between the two [art and science]? As a whole we tend to shuffle art and science into different compartments. We identify as either artists or scientists, as if allowing the two to cross paths will lead to imminent catastrophe . . . like a zombie apocalypse.

At least until the mid-to-late nineteenth century, most artists were scientists and vice versa. Indeed the word 'scientist' (much loathed at the time of its coining for the irregularity of its etymology!) is a relatively recent invention (c.1834). One need only think of Leonardo da Vinci, Mary Shelley, Hedy Lamarr, Samuel Morse, Beatrix Potter or Isaac Newton to recall the once-intuitive marriage of the two roles. The popular scientist Carl Sagan argued that science (once known as natural philosophy) is a way of thinking, not just a body of knowledge—reliant on the critical tension between creativity and scepticism. Sounds like art. Given the state of the world, re-uniting art and science couldn't make things any worse; it might even remind us that the human imagination has no limits.

This brings me neatly to an astonishing instance of the meshing of creativity, science and hope: brain soup. A Brazilian scientist, Suzana Herculano-Houzel, asked a very simple question of her colleagues—how many neurons are there in the brain? Herculano-Houzel (who did undergraduate studies in virology, graduate studies in the nervous system and a PhD in visual neurophysiology from the Max Planck Institute for Brain Research in Frankfurt) discovered that the reputed count of 100 billion neurons was a guesstimate. She devised a new method ('brain soup') that involves dissolving brain cell membranes in detergent (of all things) and then counting the nuclei and neurons left behind.

She found that while our brain wasn't exceptional for a primate of our relative weight and brain size, we do have more neurons in our cerebral cortex than any other creature (humans have 16.3 billion neurons in our cortex, gorillas 9, chimps 6 and elephants 5.6). Her total human neuron count was 86 billion. That is not quite the 100 billion that had been guessed at, but even if just one neuron connects with 1,000 others (which is where estimates currently lie), that means we have a minimum of 100 trillion synaptic connections. That's the equivalent to a processor that moves at one trillion bits per second. That's a whole lot of number/emotion/creative crunching. Not all brains are the same, and ours are unique and exceptional. And they should not be wasted.

Another amazing instance of science-meeting-art-meeting-hope is the proton gradient. One of the things that has always, at least for me, seemed utterly mysterious, was the 'spark of life' that saw beings emerge on this seething, volcanic, Hadean rock. In the late '80s, Mike Russell postulated—and this was one hell of an outlier theory—that undersea vents were responsible for biology emerging from geology on Earth 3-4 billion years ago. The more mainstream model holds that life on Earth began just 540 million years ago with the rise of oxygen, land plants, marine invertebrates, dinosaurs, and then eventually us—life as we know it. Marine explorers and scientists knew of the existence of acidic undersea vents, 'black smokers', but they are too hot and toxic to work as drivers of life, especially when ancient oceans were acidic anyway. It was possible that alkaline vents might theoretically have created the right soup for life to emerge but no-one had ever seen one.

When an alkaline vent was discovered in 2000—the so-called Lost City near the mid-Atlantic ridge—this wild undersea vent theory was tested. The 'energetics' crucial for the emergence of life were found. In this volcanic nursery there was not only catalysis provided by the metals present, but also proton flow across the vent system's mineral membranes because of alkaline conditions on one side and acidic sea water on the other. New chemical combinations were forged, including something like ATP, the chemical that powers all living cells. These molecules then drove the formation of amino acids and nucleotides, the building blocks for RNA and DNA—crucially, molecules that reproduce. With the addition of fatty molecules, protocells formed in the bubbles. These protocells, when added to the first enzyme cooked up in this infernal froth, harnessed energy from the proton flow. This meant the protocells could replicate and exist independently of the thermal broth. Bingo: bacteria and archaea. Life on Earth!

Life—its force, profusion and grandeur— is at the heart of all the plays in this volume. *They Saw a Thylacine*, by Justine Campbell and Sarah Hamilton of the HUMAN ANIMAL EXCHANGE, charts the end of life and the extinction of a species. *Thylacine* is a rich, beguiling story of the wars between a beast, a tracker, and a zookeeper. The image that confronts us at the start of the play is totemic: 'Smoke in my eyes'. The play is a potent plea for understanding, yet the way forward for them is obscured. The tracker and the zookeeper articulate the care that should be taken in our stewardship of this precious place but they also feel viscerally the delicate equilibrium in our world, a system tending towards decay and chaos. Alison, the zookeeper, comments that her colleagues couldn't tell the difference between a penis and a pouch on a thylacine. Many of the barriers to conservation action are gendered. Alison declares that this blindness and self-interest is the preserve of the privileged, the decision-makers, the men. The inference we draw is that this does not have to be the case.

Thylacine is a paean to the power of language, to the immediacy of vernacular, and the amazing tools of communication—word, metaphor and story—that transport, transform and transmogrify. Using little more than two interrelated yarns, this play speaks with great muscularity of the last human contact with a creature lost to us because of greed and cupidity. Campbell's and Hamilton's language imagines us back there— has us yearning for things to be different, to feel that cold and see that beauty, hear that growl, the cry, the screech across Tasmania that says hunger, that says sex, that says, 'I want more life'.

The disappearance and potential extinction of the humble Apis mellifera is the cue for Caleb Lewis' *The Honey Bees*. Here, unlike in *Thylacine*, the mode adopted is naturalism. Life is presented on a slab for us to examine, diagnose and discuss. Here is imprudence, the best of intentions (often deployed ill-advisedly), rage, trust, kindness, cruelty, the search for justice and the crippling legacy of insatiability and avarice. Here of course is a family—a core part of mimetic drama since the word was invented. Their fight is our fight; their agony, our agony. Naturalism is a Trojan horse for the smuggling in of metaphor and argumentation, and Lewis' stretch of WA farmland stands in for all of the Western industrialised First World.

We, like Joan's family, need to acknowledge that we are but pieces in an interconnected whole whose various parts we barely comprehend, let alone command. While we may think we are special, we are always interdependent with our environment. When we merchanise and monetise nature, there are costs and consequences. In *The Honey Bees*, colony collapse disorder, whether because of the aggregation of hives or the varroa mite, is the end result of greed. Disaster borne of pride is not a new message. I am reminded of the Bible's book of Hosea:

> Set the trumpet to thy mouth ... they have transgressed my covenant and trespassed against my law ... of their silver and their gold have they made idols ... they have sown the wind and shall reap the whirlwind ... the stalk hath no head; the bud shall yield no meal. (Chapter 8, verses 1-7)

Hosea was a prophet during a dismal time for Israel. Though surrounded by doom, he still believed in love's replenishment—but only once priorities were rebalanced. *The Honey Bees* is a play essentially, and intentionally, unbalanced. It demands that we think on ways to correct it, to right their wrongs and steer a sensible, sweeter, course of action than that which sees the business of feeding ourselves become beset with disease and ruination. But at least, as was observed in Proverbs 16.24: 'Pleasant words are a honeycomb, Sweet to the soul and healing to the bones'.

We begin Hannie Rayson's *Extinction* with broken bones: an accident in which a tiny rare creature is caught under a luxury motor car. Elemental forces then play out in a naturalistic fashion, in a thriller genre, mixing humour, intrigue, despair, fury, love and sex, tenderness and frailty. Humans are pitted against the thing they should not confront: life itself. When science, government or business sets itself apart from and above nature, or spies a landscape's resources as something to be extracted and sold (with inevitable waste dumping alongside); when we conquer and colonise; carve up or cut down; take without giving; we run into trouble. *Extinction*'s quartet of arrogant, smart and blinkered characters sure run into trouble. Rayson's special skill is in capturing the fluidity of thought and the black humour of those who seek to use language, hypocrisy and cant to win at all costs. There are no villains or heroes here: just people in all their contradictory, short-sighted glory, striving to do what they think is right.

What the play does so cleverly is to play with our sense of empathy: who or what is right? While we may wring our hands at the loss of a quoll (or a thylacine, or a honey bee), unless we take heed it will be our own extinction soon enough. This play is that taking heed. The hope glimpsed in *Extinction* is not in a character, a course of action, a phrase or even an idea (though the play of course has all of those things and more), but a reminder of our ability to laugh at ourselves, at our bad behaviour and wilful foolishness. No matter how pompous or grasping or unthinking we become, humour can cut through bombast and righteousness like a scalpel. Aristotle argued that comedy was more frivolous than tragedy. Yet Rayson, like a few other highly skilled modern playwrights, knows that colliding humour and suffering, tragic pathos with sudden glory, delivers meaning, relief and profundity through the revelation of the heroic, the ridiculous and the corrupt.

So, impossible things have happened before on this planet. Life did find a way in the most unlikely, most hostile, of circumstances. And if life can emerge from volcanic soup, and if the human brain is the most interconnected thing—ever—then maybe we can save this planet. With words, with the right balance, with laughter. Each of these plays urges us to think on the costs and benefits of current actions, past misdeeds, and our very real potential to save the world. We have done impossible things. We will continue to do impossible things. Impossibility is a species less endangered than you might think.

Chris Mead
December 2016

Chris Mead is a director and dramaturg. He is currently the Literary Director of Melbourne Theatre Company.

THEY SAW A THYLACINE

Justine Campbell
and Sarah Hamilton

JUSTINE CAMPBELL is a director, writer and actor and is co-artistic director and co-producer of HUMAN ANIMAL EXCHANGE. In 2016, their co-production with Malthouse Theatre of the award-winning *They Saw a Thylacine* toured throughout Australia. Justine's work as a writer includes *Back from the Dead Red* (Melbourne Fringe), *The Dust and Us* (La Mama) and *Untold* which was co-written with Sarah Hamilton for MTC as part of Cybec Electric. In 2015 Justine was a participant in MTC's Women Directors Program as well as Theatre Works' Directors Lab. A member of the Green Room Awards independent theatre panel, Justine's awards include: Stand Out Performer Awards NZ Fringe (2014), Green Room Award Best Female Performer in an Independent Production (2010) and Equity ACT Green Room Award for Professional Performer (2007).

SARAH HAMILTON is a Melbourne-based performer and writer and is co-artistic director of HUMAN ANIMAL EXCHANGE. Sarah's work as a writer/performer includes *A Donkey and a Parrot* (Melbourne, Adelaide and Edinburgh Fringe Festivals), *The Dust and Us* (La Mama) and *They Saw a Thylacine*. *Thylacine* premiered at Melbourne Fringe in 2013 where it was awarded Best Performance, as well as the Tiki Tour Ready award. The play toured to NZ and Adelaide Fringe Festivals and was nominated for three Green Room Awards: Best Writing, Best Female Performers and Best Production. After a collaboration with Malthouse Theatre in 2015, *They Saw a Thylacine* will tour nationally through Performing Lines in 2016. Sarah and her co-collaborator Justine Campbell recently wrote *Untold*, which was developed as part of Melbourne Theatre Company's Cybec Electric play reading series.

They Saw a Thylacine was first produced with Melbourne Fringe Festival at North Melbourne Town Hall, on 20 September 2013, with the following cast:

    ALISON REID   Justine Campbell
    BEATIE MCCULLOCH   Sarah Hamilton

Creators, Justine Campbell and Sarah Hamilton
Lighting Designer, Nick Merrylees

This play was written with the support of the Manhattan Theatre Club in partnership with the Alfred P. Sloan Foundation.

CHARACTERS

BEATIE MCCULLOCH, a thylacine tracker
ALISON REID, a zookeeper

SETTING

The play is set in Tasmania during the 1930s.

THE SIGHTING

BEATIE: Smoke in my eyes
    Oh smoke in my eyes
    Smoke blows nor-nor-east
    It's a clear night, one where you know stars can see you
    And it'll be a cold one
    Yesseee
    I chuck possum onto fire
    Fur's strung up tight
    She screamed a lot before I grabbed her
    Whacked her over head with rock
    Skun her
    Thanks for fur, Poss. Thanks for meat, Poss. Sorry about death, Poss
    Did it quick as poss, Poss
    Fire spits at me, crackin whip at me, telling me yarns with her quick wit
    You're burning up good
    Did I tell you story about Sydney, Poss?
    Over the strait, tucked well away from here
    She's bigger, warmer, they're building bloody big bridge and you can go anywhere
    Wouldn't that be …
    And in my dreamin, in my salivatin, in my smoke-blown eyes
    I see you
    Flirtin with smoke
    I can see you
    Heart goes to throat
    What do you call that?
    Here

I lean into fire and tear a limb off Poss
Feelin generous and shittin my dacks
Must be stars
Have some possum
You take it!
The tiger I'm here for the tiger that calls me this far and invites herself to dinner

DAD'S DEMISE

ALISON: Dad hears it first
The flutter of feathers
Squawking of the birds
And there's the sound of cage doors metallic swift
I shift from the table
Dad's already up from his chair
Grabbing the lamp
   'Sounds like something fishy's going on
   Up there with the birds
   I'm going to take a look'
And he's already out the door
Keys fastened round his belt
I felt like asking
Can I come too?
But I knew he'd get all gruff
   'Might be tough out there
   Not for you'
So I stand loitering by the door
There's a sound like screeching
Then nothing more
For ten whole minutes
I stand there stiff

Running through my head
What the squawking could be
Maybe a bush rat
Got into an aviary
Probably that's all
It's been quite a while
Nothing more to be heard
So I sit back down in my kitchen seat
And it's just when I've relaxed that I hear it
Heart skips a beat
There's the sound of shouting
Men
I waste no time
Grab my penknife
Head out the back door
I can hear the shouts coming
From the south part of the park
But I've got to make my way carefully
I've no lamp
Dad's got it
And it's dark
I hear the sound of clanging
A man's voice comes through
But it's muffled thick
Then the sound of chain hitting something
And that man's voice howling again and again
Footsteps running then
Nothing
Dad I yell as I start to run
Dad
I'm hurtling down the path
Headed to the outer wall of the zoo

Past the big oak
Round the corner of the track
And through the black as Newgate's knocker
The wall looms up
And with it the caretaker's gate
Always locked
But in Dad's haste to reach the noise
He's left it just ajar
Poised
One push and I'm into the zoo
Careering through the park
Past the panther, koalas and baboons
Heading right at the water feature
I hear the racoons squealing
But as I run past I realise it's me
A few more yards
I'm nearly there
I race towards the parrots' aviary
Round the corner of the cages
And what greets me is
Bad
Dad's curled up
Not moving
Next to him
The lamp's been tipped
Flames around it getting higher
So I grab Dad's legs
Widening the gap between him and the fire
Then I run back to the lamp
Set it right
And stamp out the flames till there's nothing alight
But I keep stamping

And out of the corner of my eye
At least fifty yards away
I see two figures hoicking themselves over the wall
With what looks like a net
But now they've disappeared
Nothing at all to be seen
But Dad
Doubled over on his side
The door to our precious South American macaw
Swinging wide
And me
Still stamping my feet
I kneel down by my father
Can you hear me?
He groans
Turns his head
And I let out a cry
There's a pool
Red
Oozing out from his eye

THE OLD SNOZ

BEATIE: Mornin sun bleeds into Deadman's Creek
    She shivers in a ripple and I drink
    It's too cold to be kind
    I strip for a dip with local platypus
    She's fresh by God—phwoah!
    Snow ain't common in these parts
    And I'm grateful she's graced us
    Because it's making trackin
    Easy

No crafty bugger can hide in this bush
No sireee

Kicking last night's fire in place
I see your leftover bones
You're not keen on marrow
Tige
Like the fleshy bits on the outside
And with that kick of dust n snow
I salute the poss who gave herself to us
At snow glance I see Tige's gone nor-west
Headed for the fence
I'm recknin
See you there
I'm fucken freezin
Gotta get these legs movin quick
For today and tomorrow and tomorrow
Get you to Wynyard
I check rucksack for rope
And I'm hopin it's just the right length
I'll loop you gentle and walk you to town
Won't they holler and cheer
That'll be a bloody sight for sore eyes!
A tree branch whacks my head, pounding cheek, whipping sight with ice

It's not long before the snow melt has me losing you
Crafty Tige
Did you up and fly, girl?
Is that your game, girl?
You got mystic powers ey
Like dark night's gaze
I'm reckoning you're a loner, just young and not settled down

Well I'm gonna take you to the zoo, Tige, where you'll be fed n
   full n famous
N I'll have more than poss and taties to keep me warm at night
Ain't that a thought! Ain't that bloody grand!
And in my head I'm getting ahead of my own feet
I've lost your tracks for sure now
But I don't change direction
I follow the old snoz
Got it from the Ol Man and I won't give up on it now
You'll come again with a winking head and tail flick
You'll say, *'Don't worry, I'm with her'*
And I'll say, *Lay down your guns, we mean no harm*
I'm here to collect my prize
The money, all of it thank you very much sir
Yes, that's right sir, I brought you what you sought
Yes, that's right sir, I'm a woman and I'm wearing a skirt

TAXIDERMY

ALISON: You'd think you don't have to have gone to Yale
   To know the difference 'tween
   A tiger with a penis
   And a tiger with a pouch
   But there it is
   They didn't know
   The men who captured her
   They'd named her Benjamin
   We called her Ben
   Soon as I saw her I knew
   Soon as she stepped out of the crate
   See Dad was curator
   At Beaumaris Zoo in Hobart

And I'd grown up there
Me, Alison Reid
Trade taxidermy
But while at the zoo
Dad taught me all he knew
Though in the nineteen thirties
Knowledge wasn't the only thing to get you through
See I couldn't pick up where Dad left off
Because of my tits
Tiny as they are
They wouldn't take me as far as I needed to go
And I needed to go into the zoo
But I didn't have a cock
So I didn't get a key
And I think that's what stopped me
Which in turn led to a chain of events
That saw the demise of a fair few beasts
Including Ben
But back then who knew
Our last living thylacineee
Captive Tassie tiger
Would cease to exist

BLOODY BIG DITCH

BEATIE: You're leadin me further further
    And further
    The whistlin wind persistent in my ear now
    Curls round my chin like a cold snake
    Chokin me for fear
    Nuzzlin deep, hoping for strength to
    Throttle me good

And that's when I hear it
Yip yip yip
Hear it
On the wind
Not far though I'm thinkin, not far
And there it is
Double the sound
YIP and then YIP and then YIP and then YIP
It's all my might I use not to YIP back and shout
STAY WHERE YOU ARE, TIGRESS BEAUTY BEASTY THYLACINE,
I'M COMIN AND WE'LL BE DANDY FINE YOU KNOW!
The runaway mind of a runaway girl
Knows no boundaries
You're leadin me further further further fur—
Sludge of snow slides
Down
Splintering
Spiral
Of down
Legs collapse
Beneath me
Wood snaps shut above me
Bum slams into dolerite
Ouch
A bloody big ditch
Where have you led me?
Above me around me
Man-cut wood
Needles of sky above
Sides too high
And by bloody God

I am

In

A trap

I've fallen into HER bloody trap

Who else is onto this girl?

BLOODY BASTARD DICK MOLES

And the surge of energy that hits me right now is stronger than steel

I grab rope from rucksack and throw it

Throw it

Throw it through the hatch overhead!

I hang from it, pullin with both arms and makin myself heavy as possible

And fucken heave down on the man-made roof which has me covered in everythin

Hold breath, hold breath tight and close eyes sharp and pound pound pound the head and kick kick kick like the wind and her cold snake

HOT ROPE PULLS MY HANDS TILL IT BURNS

I've got to hold on for dear—

And down comes the stupid trap roof till I can see my way out, climbin walls for sheer joy and escape is my victory—YIP YIP YIPPPPPEEEEEEEEEE!!!!!!

I'm not beat and I eat

Some possum

For sheer delight

BRUCE LIPSCOMBE

ALISON: Bruce Lipscombe is the superintendent
    Of the Reserves Committee
    And it's because of him
    Things start to get shitty

Now Bruce is a man who cares
About the bottom line
If he has to cut a man's nose
To shave a pound or two
He has no qualms—that's just fine
So when Bruce heard the news
That the zoo's curator
My father
Was badly beaten on the job
There was no offer of a few bob's worth of compensation
Not one visit for the duration of Dad's stay in hospital
When my father saved the macaw and took the hit
Bruce Lipscombe didn't give a shit

A TALL SHADOW

BEATIE: Break o'day wakes me with a slap

    Not a foul slap—the slap says *'Congratulations! You are alive! Well done! What a bloody blighter! Have courage! There's a thylacine out there all for you and ain't that bloody grand!'*

    And the morning's optimism makes me want to slap it right back and say

    Oh thanks but I'm hurtin and my feet are bleedin and my love is gone

    But my snoz tells me that's the worst I can do

    For that

    Will

    Hurt

    The

    Most

    So I strip off and wet myself in creek

    For pain and pleasure

    Winter sun gurgles a grin on my naked back

And the grin snaps shut
A tall shadow
With a hat
I lay flat in water
Not breathin
Nostrils just out of water for fear of drownin
My blankets are on the rocks and rucksack too. Oh don't see them please don't see them, should have covered them in leaves. What a fool. What a bloody fool. Have I learned nothing?
Nude in the bush with nuthin but a stubborn head
The cold is not a problem
I am numb
Lie here and watch the clouds making shapes above my camp
They look different through the water and tell me there's rain headed this way
Who is this shadow? Is it looking for me or her?
And will it JUST PISS THE BUGGER FUCK OFF
And leave me to my fray
I hear a cough and a kick
It's a man
And I'm not movin yet
I am not
For the findin
Lay here till I am burnin
And ears have lost all
But the babble of creek and snigger of wind
Shut eyes
Burnin
Burnin
Chest exploding
Wait for more
I can't, I can't anymore

The rocks catch my feet as I edge this body
Out of creek
Face to feet
All I can see is me
Pink and blue
Shrivelled prune
Crank my chin forward
To face this fucker
But he's not there
He's not here anywhere
Musnt'v seen me
Behind these trees
Face-up floating in creek
Slowly slowly wrap myself in warm
Cannot move very well at all
Am tempted by the relief
To stay put
But must
Move
Or death will take all that is left
And fuck that for a joke!
Joke's on you, Beatie, joke's on you
That's me—I'm Beatie, did you know that?
Well you probably didn't because I did not introduce
Meself through the smoke

THE OUTCOME

ALISON: It's five years past since Dad was hit by those two thugs
    He's still the man in charge of the zoo
    But in saving our macaw
    He lost his left eye

And the wound's turned cancerous
So we know he will die ... quite soon
Now I'm doing most of the work
It's not a responsibility that I shirk
I was born a zookeeper's daughter
I oughta be curator too
I oughta be officially running this zoo
But that's not the case cos of you know who—Bruce Lipscombe
Dad receives a letter from Superintendent Bruce and his wingman Brain
Bruce and Brain, what a pair
Two guys who feign to give a shit
Two guys who feign to care
They seize upon Dad's cancer
As an opportunity to reduce
The expenses of running the zoo
Present him with a proposal
The disposal of his job
They want him to become a part-time officer only
Reducing his income by over a third
Their thanks for his dedication to his work
This guy Bruce Lipscombe is a real jerk
So Dad refuses and counters their offer
That his daughter Alison
Me aged thirty-one
Should take charge of the zoo
Become the new curator
Being paid less than half
What is my due
And Dad'll resign
Work alongside me for free

To help the transition
In every capacity
It's a pretty good deal
It's a bloody good deal
But the board rejects it
Shit
Their official line
> *'We want to be seen to appoint openly and fairly*
> *Any hint of nepotism is clearly*
> *Something to be steered well away from, my dear'*
This is what I'm told
Same old lies
For Bruce Lipscombe is the third Lipscombe
On the Reserves Committee

But man is a different beast	But man is a different beast
Made for the hunt	Chomping at the bit
So different rules apply	So different rules apply
To those with a cock	To those with a cock
Than to those with a cunt	Than to those with a clit *

LOOKIN UP

BEATIE: The afternoon takes me to waterfalls
    Upon waterfalls
    Upon waterfalls
    And I could just float on down
    All the way to
    Hobart Town
    Dash my brains out on the rock
    Tear a hole in my frock

---

* In productions where young audiences are involved, performers may feel it more appropriate to use this alternative text.

Call to the heavens
What is left for me?
And out in front I see wallaby
Wallaby all three
Little joey with head pokin out
I grab rock
And pelt it at their
Pretty heads
Missin all three
Dinner hops away and
Taties rattle emptily

Eyes to where rock has landed
There's blood
It paves its way through snow
Away from wallaby all three
It's headed nor-nor-west
I drop to knees and see
Another bloody trappers trap
This has teeth
And teeth marks
And left fur
And there's your colour
And your
And your bloody paw prints
Padded through snow
I will not lose you
Retrieve thrown rock
Clasp in hand
Concealed
You're my secret weapon

I will throw it at his head

At temple
At back of neck
I'll scrape it down his spine
And force him to his knees
How dare he take you
How dare he scare me
How dare he dare to breathe

DAD

ALISON: Dad dies December thirteenth nineteen thirty-five
Bruce Lipscombe takes over running the zoo
Till a new curator can be found
And now that Dad's dead
Bruce takes his chance
   'Unfortunately, my dear,
   There's no two ways about it
   We the board are prepared to let you and your mother
   Stay in the zookeeper's cottage for free
   But that means you're here to help me
   Whenever I need
   You know how this place works
   And what needs to be done
   So while we wait for a new curator
   I'm prepared to concede the cottage
   But in exchange you will give your services
   Whenever required'
He takes Dad's keys
   'I'll drop them off each morning
   And pick them up at five'
If it weren't for this bureaucracy
Ben might still be alive

And I can see how things will now be at the zoo
It won't be the same here Dad
Without you

LYING TO THE MAN

BEATIE: The fence
Man-made from steel
Catches me early
Much earlier than
Old man told me
It would
Your prints are less bloody
And I'm hopin you're recoverin
From the arse-wipe's teethy trap
Lookin up I see the only way is down

Sarah Hamilton as Beatie in Melbourne Fringe Festival's 2013 production of THEY SAW A THYLACINE. *(Photo: Pia Johnson)*

It's a bloody steep ravine
Fence reaching deep
He made it well
Old man
And it's a bum job
You've gotta scoot down in the snow
You've gotta scoot down on ya bum
To get to the bottom. Ha!
And scootin and draggin and singin
I like the flowers I like the daffodils I like the mountains I like the rollin
   'What you doing, lad?'
Stop. Heart in throat
I'm just lookin at this fence, doin some maintenance
   'Look at me, kid'
I turn slowly
I'm a mess but sure I'm all woman
He stops, tall in front me, only halfway down ravine
He's got black hat black coat
Ripped trousers
And he looks about as stuffed as me
   'What ya singin?'
Bout the mountains
   'Ya seen any mountains?'
Ah, yes sireee, I've seen plenty
   'I'm huntin tha thylacine, ya seen him?'
No.
Lumpy throat gargles in my ears and how could it be?
   'Well, he's just down there see, he copped an injury and now'
You're trapped
There's a ditch at the bottom and the fence funnels into a dead end

You're trapped
It's got you at the bottom of ravine
And wallaby, wallaby tied to fence to lure you
Struggling still-live wallaby
That clever bloody mongrel man
And now I see
I have you
Ears pricked
Caught in my stare
Here you are
And here is he
With his bleedin big gun and all
I gots
Rucksack n rope

And behind man
Is
I cannot say
I cannot breathe too much
Because he'll see
Because behind man
Heart in throat
Lady Tige
Is your flippin mate
Standing strong
Dark stripes tall
Got you
In his eye
And I just want to propel rock at man's hatted head
And scream *RUN RUN AWAY YOU CRAZY TIGER BOY*
GET AWAY FROM ME
OR I'LL CHUCK MY BLOODY ROCK AT YOU

AND EAT YOU FOR MY TEA
And that's what goes through my head
Till I look up and out and see
Your striped other half
He's off
Dark as shadow
Heading behind the forest wall
Away from fence
And
You
Lady Tige
Stuck at bottom
Not a yip

THE FIRING

ALISON: There once was a set of zookeepers
    Henry, Bill and Dick
    They got sacked one day
    No residual pay
    Because Bruce Lipscombe is a prick
    Now Bill, Dick and Henry
    Are well-trained men
    Been here ten years
    Keepers with knowledge and know-how
    But Bruce and Brain
    Boot them out
    See, it's the Depression
    There's no drought when it comes to manual labour
    There's no shortage of men
    And they figure
        'Doesn't take much to open and close a gate

Throw some meat in a cage'
So they get six guys from the work-for-the-dole
And don't have to worry about giving them a wage
They plan to tighten things up
Run this place on the cheap
So Bill, Dick and Henry are turned out
And in their place
A bunch of men
Who
No doubt
Need jobs but don't care two hoots about the zoo
They do what suits them
So time and again
Our beasts begin to go without
They don't unlock our panther's
Sleeping quarters for the night
And within weeks
He's a sight for sore eyes
Two days later he dies
Pneumonia

TRUTH BE TOLD

BEATIE: *I'll help you, sir*
  I've got length of rope
  See
  To tie around her neck
  I'm Beatie, daughter of McCulloch
  And truth be told
  I'm here to take Tige away
  Too
  To Jimmy in Wynyard

Then she's headed south
To Beaumaris Zoo
I've been trackin her for days
And here we are
Shall we cut it fifty each way?
  'Well ain't you a trick
  You funny little Beatie Bo Peep
  Watcha gunna do with that there rope?
  He ain't that obedient'
Sir, I believe it's a she
Can tell by her muzzle
  'Couldn't tell by yours at first
  Little Bo Peepy'
I don't like your tone, sir
Please refrain from callin me
Bo Peepy
I'm Beatie
Daughter of McCulloch
  'Well Miss Beatie
  Trixie Belle
  I'm here for my thylacine
  Too
  So I guess we got no choice
  But to share her, me and you'
You not gonna shoot her are you?
What's ya name?
  'Alfred
  You can call me Fred if your feelin like it
  I'm Alfred, son of Alfred'
You Alfred Alfred?
  'No just Alfred'
Fred. You're not gunna shoot her are ya?

> *'Well I'm still formulatin my plan*
> *Beaty Trix*
> *And I'm hopin to get the most*
> *Bang*
> *For my buck'*
> Me too Fred. Alfred. An we gonna get the most
> Keepin her alive
> *And fixin up her foot*
> *They your traps out*
> *Cross the plains?*
> > *'What's it to you, Trix B?'*
> *I fell in one*
> *And Tige's got hobble*
> *Don't think it's the best way to catch a thylacine*
> > *'Well ain't you a funny girl*
> > *What you think about them wallaby bait?'*
> *What you think about the fence my old man made?*
> > *'You yanky my chain, girlo*
> > *This fence been here longer than*
> > *Mountains*
> > *Or so I been told*
> > *And it's well-known*
> > *It's legend*
> > *It's right on the boundary'*
> *Ol man made it*
> *And mapped it*
> *N here I am, see?*

THE MAN WITH ONE ARM

ALISON: Not long after the firing
    I start to hear it regular

THEY SAW A THYLACINE

The yip yip yap
Of Ben in the dark
Meaning she's been locked out of her den
Got nowhere to park
Herself away from the cold
I'm told there's a man with one arm
Braithwaite
He's got the job of unlocking the gate
To let her into her den
So one morning
I loiter by Ben's cage
It's a fucking mess
He hasn't mucked it out
When he turns up I see why
This guy's a lout
His whole look
From his shoes to his hair
Screams
   'I could care less
   About being here
   One arm or not
   I don't give a rot'
You in charge of unlocking the pen
So Ben can get into her den after dark?
He looks me up and down
   'If I am, what's it to you?'
I don't mean to tell you what to do
It's too cold to be leaving
This tiger out the freeze
   'Please
   They's used to the cold

I'm told
She'll be jake'
Her yippin's keepin me awake
So I know that's not the case
In the wild they've got a sheltered den
Which is why
You need to unlock the pen every day
He stands there silent
   'Get out of my way'
I can see this guy
Isn't going to try
To see my point of view
I'll need to contact Bruce Lipscombe
All I can do
See if he'll give me
Dad's spare set of keys
And that thought strikes
A feeling of unease

LOOPING TIGE

BEATIE: And all this commotion
   This negotiatin n hopin
   Has given you plenty of time to eat
   Tige
   T' gather up your strength
   But your dinner sits slowly dying
   And you haven't taken up the offer
   Too stuck to partake
   In this dead-end dinner date
   You can't get out
   Lady Tige,

Without comin past us
Me and Fred
This strange bush gent
With his hat and his coat and
His gun slowly bent
Off his arm and lowered to ground
He's meanin me no harm
He's tellin me now
And I says we've got to do this together
What's he gonna do, shoot me and take her
Or shoot her and take me?
No good either way

I'll have 'em both instead

And I keep good and quiet about Tiger Boy
To Fred

>*'You dreamin, Bea*
>*Let's get this Tige*
>*To Post Office Tree*
>*Then we'll hitch a ride to*
>*The coast*
>*Are you with me, Trixee?'*

Yes, I'm with him
I got meself no choice in matters
And he seems fine enough
For a filthy trapper
I'm a tracker
And there's a difference tween him n me
I tell Fred about the fire and the sharin of bones
I tell him about how you, Lady Tige, don't mind me
Bein round

I tell Fred bout me Dad
Bout Sydney
I tell him that I'm plannin
To skip this island
Make my way to
Where it's bigger, warmer and
Full of possibility

And while I'm talkin
Fred's listnin
Makin cracks and callin names
I'm pulling rope from rucksack
And coiling it round my hand
It's tight n proper-fitted
Knotted for grip and strength
I make a lasso for you, Tige
Don't worry
Tige
I'll hold you gentle
And Fred won't hurt you
Less you hurt me
Fred takes rope too
From his own rucksack
He's back up I tell him
I'm the chief
 'You're the chief, Beatie Trix
 I'm gonna let you tame the beast
 Then we'll march her inta town
 I've got ma gun so don't chew
 Worry, cos I'm backup man'
I could kick him in the head and dash his guts with rock
But I do not

He seems
He'll do for the job

I climb down ravine
Towards you
Slowly
Tige
Down snow
Down fence
And you don't seem to mind
I've whispered to you night and day
Girl
And you must a heard
You flash your teeth at me
And yelp
   '*I'll Shoot! I'll SHOOT!*'
Hold your flippin gun, Fred,
She's not gonna bite
HOLD YOUR GUN DOWN ON THE GROUND
STAND ON IT, DO NOT TOUCH IT WITH YOUR HANDS
Fred. Alfred.
   '*Woah, girl. Woah, Trixie bell.*'
It's Beatie. Daughter of McCulloch.
And I got this covered.

You do not call my bluff, girl, and nor does he
I take both hands and drop the loop wide around your slender
   shoulders
And you are letting me you are letting me
WHAT A DINKUM BLOODY LEGENDARY THYLACINEEE
I pull tight on rope, not to choke
Harness you for the walk
To Post Office Tree

Hadn't thought of that meself
Glad Fred suggested
Tall bloomin likeable Fred

He offers me his hand and pulls me up and out
He's holding me tight
While I'm holding your rope tight in the other
You might be thinkin I trust him
Tige
And to be fair I
Don't
But I've got to play along here
Because losing you is not
On my plate

ASKING BRUCE

ALISON: I ask Bruce Lipscombe
    For Dad's spare set of keys
    He says no

LOOPING TIGE

BEATIE: It's quite a journey, Tige
    And my rope is long
    If you keep pulling
    That way and this
    You're going to choke
    I'll keep it loose
    But you must walk with me
    Hobble out front
    Lick your paw clean, girl
    Keep it like that till we get you to the zoo

They'll fix ya up
And for now the snow'll keep it numb
I'll roast you
A poss
Tige
I'll serve one up for tea
When we get to Post Office Tree

Fred's gettin the idea
Out front
Dropping wallaby guts in the snow
Every hundred feet or so
Salvaged them from the fence, see
He'll run out fore long
But he's got you on side
And what a fucken sight
We must be
Us three
With your silent witness
Followin behind

ASKING BRAIN

ALISON: I think to myself, *If Bruce Lipscombe*
Is going to keep the keys and remain
Unhelpful
Perhaps I'll have more luck with sidekick Brain
Fingers crossed behind my back
I open Brain's office door
I'm trying to use all my restraint
I'd like to lodge a formal complaint
I hear myself say

In a voice that sounds just like … mine
He looks up and coughs
   'Well certainly let's talk
   Take a seat'
He offers the chair opposite
Sits himself up
Taps his feet
Shuffles his papers
Grabs a pen
   'Tell me what's happened
   With whom
   And when'
It's to do with Ben
   'Ah the tiger
   What's the problem with her now?'
She was locked out of her den last night
Fifth night in a row
   'That's not good
   Not good at all
   Who's supposed to unlock her gate?'
Braithwaite
   'The man with one arm
   I'll speak to him myself
   Leave it with me
   Let's dispense with the formality of paperwork
   It's not that I shirk my duties
   It's just better face-to-face
   There's a way to do things here
   A time and a place
   I'm sure you're aware how it is these days, my dear
   We've got so few staff

There's so much to do
Sure, it's not good
If the tiger's left out
For a night or two
Leave it with me'
And he stands
Motions for the door
I'm not leaving yet
I look to the floor
What I would appreciate
Is my own set of keys
My father had a spare set
　'Yes, pet, and it's all very sad
　But times have changed
　There's a new protocol to be had
　You're already still living in the caretaker's cottage
　And Bruce Lipscombe is in charge
　Till we find a resident keeper
　He'll keep the keys
　Just leave it with me
　Whadaya say?'
And there's nothing I can
Cos it's nineteen thirty-six
I'm a woman
And he's a man

FRED'S SIREN

BEATIE: The wet of this snow melt
　　Has creeks gushing into rivers
　　We stop
　　Rucksacks to ground
　　And drink

I wonder if he saw me
Floatin in the creek
   'Nah I did not see you floatin in the creek
   What do you think I am?
   Some kind of perverted man?
   I did stumble across a siren
   In the forest
   A maiden so fair
   She was not wearing underwear
   I did see a girl with hair
   Ballooning silky smooth
   I did see that
   But, I did not see you'
And the bastard winks at me

THE STORM—PART ONE

ALISON: I wake with a jolt
   A wail piercing the cottage walls
   She's crying through the dark
   A yap yap whimper
   Not a bark—eighth night in a row
   Damn that man
   I think as I shrug on my shawl
   Pull on my slippers
   Head down the hall
   That no good 'zookeeper'
   On the work-for-the-dole
   Even after Brain has spoken to him
   He's left Ben locked out of her den
   She's been exposed to this freezing winter

Time and again
She's caged at the back of the zoo
Away from the office
Storeroom and hullabaloo
Of the more popular animals
And she's being neglected
Left out night after night
Cos she's far from the madding crowd
Far out of sight
He doesn't bother to unlock the sheltered part of her den
Like he's been told
And now she's crying
To get some warmth
Fuck
It's cold

POST OFFICE TREE

BEATIE: It's dark when we reach Post Office Tree
    She's a welcome sight
    Silly ol stump on the side of the road
    With tin billy for post
    We've travelled too low for snow
    And ain't that the relief for our poor frozen toes

    I tie you to branch next to Post Office Tree
    With some moss underneath for you to lie
    Rest up
    Fred makes fire and heads for water
    From nearby creek
    I think he's gone swimmin too cos he comes back
    Different
    Hair swept wet to one side

Less grubby and his chubby chin
Tucks into his neck which is
Undone from his buttoned-up coat
He grins like a dickhead
And I grin back too
We made it bloody heck
This far with you
Tige
And I'm that close to tellin him
Bout your mate, girl
But I don't cos I'm hopin
He'll keep following you
And then we'll get double
Bang for buck
 'Post'll be here in the mornin, Trix
 So snuggle in tight for tonight
 I'll be here by the fire
 And you're welcome to warmth too
 Trixie Bell Bo Peepy
 Trixie Dixie'
Don't call me that ya fool
I'm no Bo Peeper
I've got my blankets and here I'll lay
G'night, bushwacker cray
 'G'night, fair maiden of the forest night'
Shut ya trap ya wobbly goose

And I close eyes and nearly forget
Tiger Boy's on the loose
And you're on a noose

THE STORM—PART TWO

ALISON: I make a snap decision
   I've got to break into the zoo
   And somehow get her out
   Of this ghastly night air
   If I had Dad's spare set of keys
   It would all be okay
   But I don't I say
   Out loud as I push my way through
   The back door
   A blast of wind
   Hits me right in the face
   As I shrug off my slippers

Sarah Hamilton (left) as Beatie and Justine Campbell as Alison in Melbourne Fringe Festival's 2013 production of THEY SAW A THYLACINE. *(Photo: Pia Johnson)*

And in their place
Pull on my gumboots
Striding out into the dark
Through the howling of the wind
I hear her howling
Through her cage
And the rage I feel
Spurs me on through the back garden
And I begin to run
Pushing into the rain
Heading to the outer wall of the zoo
When above I hear a snap
From out of nowhere there's a thud
Back of my neck
And I fall to the ground sliding into the mud
For a moment I'm stunned
Dazed with the pain
My face is pressed into the dirt
I raise my arm to feel the back of my head
My hair is drenched from the force of the rain
And the force of the branch
Where it fell has left a split in my scone
I can feel a sharp stinging
From the cracking thud
As the split and the hair
Congeal with the blood with the blood with the blood
It's not too deep
I can tell
As I pick myself up
Survey the branch where it fell
It's large it's large—not too large not too large

I know I'll be fine
But this time I tread more carefully
On the path leading to the wall
I'm already drenched
And that momentary rush of adrenalin
I felt when I woke
Is waning
The pain in my head
Is strong is strong
Won't be long before I choke
Damn that lazy heartless bloke
I hear Ben call out
She'll be drenched
Chilled to the bone
I head past the big oak
Round the corner of the track
I can see the outline of the wall
And I hear her call
She's just on the other side
Locked in her front cage
I reach the caretaker's gate
And give it a shake
Though I know there's no use
A string of abuse escapes my mouth
You wanna know what I said?
It rhymes with 'brass hole'
Yes that's what I yelled and more
See the wall's a good seven foot high
It's gotta be
It's a zoo
We know why

It's to keep the crazies out
Well this crazy's going in
So I pull off my boots
Hoist up my nightie
And I stick my foot through the little gap
In the wrought-iron gate
The steel is slippery
Cuts into my socks
As I get towards the top
The wrought iron
Rocks off one of its hinges
The gate lunges backwards
My foot slips free
And I'm grasping it
With all my might
But I feel the other hinge
Beginning to go
And I know that if I don't let go
The gate's gonna break and so might my neck
So I bend my left knee
And swing myself free
And I squat on the outside of the wall as the rain pelts me hard
Down my head my neck my spine
Through the roar of the wind
I hear Ben whine
Just hang on, Ben,
Just make it through till dawn
And tomorrow I'll come straight to you
But all I can do is turn around and make my way
Back through the wind and the snow
My heart feels tight like it's being squeezed

I miss you, Dad
The goddamn goddamn goddamn keys

WALLOPED

BEATIE: The post office wagon wakes me with a clap
Postie leers down at me
Grinning like a fat wombat
Scratches his groin
Rubs his knee
Calls me missy
I swallow morning spit and store it
Deep in throat for launching at his face
If I hafta do it
I'll slit his throat and kick his testes
If he dare mess with me
Or you, Tigress Mighty Queen
Yip yip yip, you call
Hollering for your mate
But the hills ignore you
Just the wind
Whips her curling snake
And you don't stop yippin
    'SHUT HER THE DEVIL UP' yells Postie
Fred tells him I'm a lady and to be treated as such
And Postie laughs his head off
And you yip and yip and yip
And Postie laughs and laughs and laughs
And Fred wallops him on the face
What have ya done, FRED?
Who's gonna drive us to town, FRED?
Fred's gone red. Beet red.

He tells me he'll be takin' us to town
And Postie's comin too

You've stopped your yippin now, you've barked yaself hoarse
And I feel I could nearly scoop ya up in these arms of mine
And in my dreamin, in my beatin, in my wanderin mind
I hear
A crash
A bang
Of wood bang against
TIGE
AGAINST YOU, LADY TIGE
WHAT ARE YOU DOIN, FRED?
    'Woah girl, woah Trixie Belle
    Gotta get her in the box, best knock her out for a bit
    Not gonna hurt her'
Fred's gun is slung from his left arm
I slide my hand beneath the leather strap
And with a quick whip
It flies off his shoulder
I take the gun hostage against Fred's back
SHE'S NOT FOR THE KILLIN, FRED
SHE'S FOR LIVING N FEEDIN N FAME
PUT DOWN YOUR LOG
He does. He picks you up, weak n limp by the scruff
You submit cos you're asleep
He walloped your head
And I will not talk to him.

He puts you in a box on back of wagon
I keep the gun

Your mate's too late

FINDING BEN

ALISON: It's a still morning when I wake
   My head throbs and stings
   I look out the window and see
   Rings of smoke coming from the office chimney
   Little specks of snow
   Are falling silently
   But the stream of Bridgewater Gerry's roaring
   And the mountain's pissed off, gone out whoring
   Forty-two degrees south

   There's no sound coming from the tiger's pen
   As I step towards the cage
   I see her on her side
   I squat down
   And call out
   Ben
   I think I see her ears flinch
   I peer at her belly
   To see if there's any movement
   There is
   Thank God she's made it through
   She lifts her head
   And it's then that one-armed Braithwaite
   Appears with the keys
       'Mighta known I'd see you here'
   Is all he says as he jangles them and unlocks the door
   He gingerly steps in
   Pulls a freshly dead rabbit
   Out from his sack
       'This should keep 'im going for a day or two'

He goes to step out
Wait
Unlock the den
   'Why?'
She was left out last night—again
   'She? Oh well they's tough ain't they?'
Unlock it—she's cold—look at her
   '... Righto'
He heads to the door of the den
And I head into the cage
Squatting next to Ben
Her breathing's shallow
Help me lift her in?
He hesitates then squats beside me
As we begin to lift her
She pushes up onto her feet
And slowly crosses the cage into the den
But her movements are swayed and stiff
Like an aged drunkard
   'She'll be jake'
Says Braithwaite
And I feel it inside
Not in me waters
Somewhere deeper
She'll be okay she will
She'll live to see another day
Braithwaite eyes me
   'What happened to your scone?'
I fell over last night
During the storm
   'Better get it seen to
   Looks like a nasty gash'

TOWARDS THE SEA

BEATIE: We travel along the wet road for
    A very long time
    Postie stirs next to me
    And you stir in the back
    Coughin and coughin and wheezin too
    An Postie calls a stop

    Postie stinks—he's been on the drink
    He's a bloody useless mess
    Fred hit him hard
    And now he's regrettin
    With Postie's frettin
    What he did to him

    I shoot Fred
    A thank-you
    For bashin Postie up
    Could've done it meself though

    Holding gun tight
    I leap into back with you, Tige
    How you goin, girl?
    You're bleedin from ya nose
    Lick it clean, girl
    You won't have to put up with much
    More
    And she looks at me like she hates me
    And ain't that a shame
    Ain't that a crying shame?

    I duck behind bushes for a piss

Can hear Postie fartin and spewin
Bloody disgustin
Mess

YIP YIP YIP
I hear ya yippin strong
Clean m'self up and head back to you
And bloody Postie too
He's in the back of the wagon
Pokin at you with a stick!
And you're snarlin at him
Snarlin and biting
And he's stabbing at you!
Stabbing at your wounded foot!
GET AWAY FROM HER, YOU USELESS PRICK
   'Woah girl, woah, Trixie Bell
   Best calm down n give the gun now please'
It's Beatrix, Fred, and no, I will not CALM DOWN
THROW THAT BASTARD OFF
I kick Fred in the shins
And this wasn't part of the plan
Gun's still in my hand
I lurch at Postie's head
He's fat but he's quick
And with his stick he whacks me in the eye
An me an you are screamin
And it's time
I kick Postie in the gonads!
Half blind half cryin
He falls back
Back
Crushin

Crushin
You, Lady Tige, and
Wood
Splintering wood
He's smashed your box
And
FLASH
LIKE A FLASH
THERE YOU GO
AWAY YOU LEAP
FROM THE CRUSHING PRISON
OVER FAT BASTARD'S HEAD
THE FLIGHT IS
HIGH
AND YOU SCREAM GOODBYE
   'SHOOT HER, BEATRIX
   SHOOT HER DEAD
   She's worth more dead
   Than gone'
But I can't I won't
She's headed away from me
She's headed towards the sea
She's taking the nor-nor-west
It's not for me
To kill you
Beauty Tigress Queen
And the yippin is deafnin
It thunders in
It claps the hills
And wakes the heavens
And the Postie hollers

And hisses
And pisses
His dacks for gonads
Are his weakness
And he won't be making any more children

Fred grabs my arms
Sees my wobbly
Knees and pleads
Me to give up the gun
He's a good shot
I can tell
And you're still visible
As living hell
Let go of me, Fred. You will not have the gun.
And he kisses me fair smack bang on the lips
I bite on his mouth
And tell him
NO YOU DON'T, ALFRED ALFRED
I AM NOT FOR THE TAKING

THE NEWS

ALISON: That afternoon
   I head back from the Royal Hobart Hospital
   Twelve stitches in tow
   I can see the smoke
   Rising from the office chimney
   I hear the drone of Brain's voice
      'We have no choice
      She'll need to know
      It'll be a shame to let
      Her services go

 We've been saving a lot'
 'They've got to leave'
Comes in Bruce's drawl
 'If I have to heave the old spinster out myself I will'
I tap on the door
Swing it wide
And there they are
The pair of them
Legs astride
 'Speak of the devil' laughs Bruce
 'Just jokes
 Good to see you, Miss Reid
 We feel the need to let you know
 That although it's slow going
 In finding a replacement for your dad
 We've had to come to a decision
 About the caretaker's cottage
 We're going to need to lease it out
 Bit of a drought on funds
 Now that we're paying your mother a small annuity
 So you see
 You'll need to vacate
 By the end of the month
 We felt it best to give you plenty of time
 To organise the move
 Some of the dole boys can give you a hand if you need'
Bruce turns and looks at Brain
 'Yes certainly—Anything we can do to help'
I stand there almost dumbstruck
Don't quite know why
I've been expecting this sly man

To make his final move
To remove our family from the zoo
I go to speak
My voice is thin
Almost sounds like a yelp
I'll let you know
Where to forward the mail
As I turn to leave
Bruce pipes up
   'Oh one last thing
   One of the visitors reported your thylacine
   Looked as if it was dead in its cage
   Braithwaite checked up on it
   Found it was true
   Sorry to have to break it to you

Justine Campbell as Alison in Melbourne Fringe Festival's 2013 production of They Saw a Thylacine. *(Photo: Pia Johnson)*

I know you were fond of it
Perhaps you can look into sourcing another?'

EYE'S A BLEEDING MESS

BEATIE: Fred scoops Postie's legs onto back of wagon
Ties him down and chucks Tige's cage on his
Tear-soaked chin
> *'He's not gonna do you no more harm, Trix*
> *Hop in, I'll take you to town*
> *Get you cleaned up*
> *You gotta get seen*
> *Your eye's a bleedin mess*
> *And you're too lean*
> *Too mean'*

And you are too assuming
FRED
Don't be talkin to me
Like that
And don't be sucking my face
Or I'll knock ya flat

Look to distant coast and you are gone

The sun whacks its head on mine
And ain't that hurtin
The curtain of strong
In bones of bones of bones
Of mine and Da's and hers
Have ached
And this is not
What I was planning
For and

Water and
Rivers
And oceans
Run down my face
And heave at my spine
And they are
Loud
Sobbing
Waterfalls
Of
Mine
All mine

THE IRONY

ALISON: Ben dies seventh September nineteen thirty-six
Six weeks earlier the Tassie tiger is declared a protected species
Mum and I move out of the caretaker's cottage
The Depression still rages
So we live with relatives
I go back to taxidermy
Bruce and Brain finally get their game plan in nineteen thirty-seven
And the zoo shuts down
It has never re-opened

THE DROWNED QUEEN

BEATIE: Fred doesn't say a word
Just sits and steers us all the way
To Wynyard
While my creakin body
Whimpers and willows

In its own pith
Of ancient disappointment

Out front of station
Fred leaves me alone
He bundles up Postie
And drags him in
    'Found 'im like this on the side of the road
    Drunk
    Out of sorts
    Hazy and chokin'
An the constables thank him
For his good deed
For saving old
Postie
From his own
Sordid mead
It's the charm, with Fred
That gets him away
With whatever he pleases
And that is not
What I like about
Him

I yank gun from skirt
And chuck it under Fred's
Seat
Too heavy and foldin
And loud
For me

I go down to beach
Sea is too far from Deadman's Creek

An the squeakin sand makes music when I walk
Like campfire singin
And spoon and fork
Bangin gainst each other
In the rhythm of silly made-up song
There's a shadow on my wool-clad back
Tall and cloaked and hatted
It's got a certain limp to it
Which wasn't there before
What you doing, Fred?
    'Trixie Bell Beatie
    I'm followin you, can't you see
    What are you doing, Lady Mystery?'
Listenin
Can you hear it?
The singing sand
Think I might be mad
It's singing
See
An we walk down the beach
Singin with pebbles crunchin
Where the creek comes to shore

And that's when we see
In the sand
Wet
Stopped
Complete
A drowned queen in the sand
Stripes pointing to the sea
Jaw gapin wide
Teeth perfect prisms

Eyes so dark rolled back in head
Foot with blood
No more

And prints in the sand
Headin away
East
East Coastally

THE END

Hannah Day (left) as Piper and Sarah McNeill as Dixon-Brown in Black Swan State Theatre Company's 2015 production of Extinction. *(Photo: Gary Marsh)*

EXTINCTION

Hannie Rayson

HANNIE RAYSON a graduate of the University of Melbourne and the Victorian College of the Arts (VCA). She holds an Honorary Doctorate of Letters from La Trobe University. Rayson was a cofounder of Theatreworks, and has served as writer-in-residence at the Mill Theatre, Playbox Theatre, La Trobe University, Monash University, VCA and New Writing North (Newcastle-upon-Tyne, UK).

Her plays have been performed extensively around Australia and several have been produced overseas. They include *Please Return to Sender*, *Mary*, *Leave It Till Monday*, *Room to Move*, *Hotel Sorrento*, *Falling from Grace*, *Scenes from a Separation* (co-written with Andrew Bovell), *Competitive Tenderness*, *Life After George*, *Inheritance*, *Two Brothers*, *The Glass Soldier* and *The Swimming Club*. Hannie's most recent play, *Extinction*, was commissioned by The Manhattan Theatre Club in New York through the Alfred P Sloan Foundation. Hannie's plays have won AWGIE Awards; Green Room Awards; Helpmann Awards; NSW Premier's Literary Awards; Victorian Premier's Literary Awards and the Age Performing Arts Award. *Life After George* was the first play ever to be nominated for the prestigious Miles Franklin Award.

Hannie's memoir, *Hello, Beautiful!*, was published by Text Publishing in February 2015. She adapted the story for a one-woman show, also called *Hello, Beautiful!*, which opened at The Malthouse Theatre in May 2016. She is touring the show nationally in 2017/18.

Hannie also writes for newspapers and magazines and in 1999 she won the Magazine Publishers' Society of Australia's Columnist of the Year Award for her column in *HQ Magazine*.

Her television scripts include 'Sloth' (ABC, 'Seven Deadly Sins') and she co-wrote two episodes of the award-winning series 'Seachange' (ABC/Artists Services). A feature film of *Hotel Sorrento* (1995) was nominated for ten Australian Film Institute Awards, winning two, including Best Screenplay Adaptation.

Extinction was first produced by Black Swan State Theatre Company at Heath Ledger Theatre, Perth, on 19 September 2015, with the following cast:

DR PIPER ROSS	Hannah Day
HARRY JEWELL	Matt Dyktynski
HEATHER DIXON-BROWN	Sarah McNeill
ANDY DIXON	Myles Pollard

Director, Stuart Halusz
Set and Costume Designer, Bryan Woltjen
Lighting Designer, Trent Suidgeest
Sound Designer and Composer, Ben Collins
Voice Coach, Luzita Fereday
Fight Director, Andy Fraser

This play was written with the support of the Manhattan Theatre Club in partnership with the Alfred P. Sloan Foundation.

CHARACTERS

DR PIPER ROSS, 30, a zoologist on secondment from the San Diego Zoo

HARRY JEWELL, 45, CEO of Powerhouse Mining

PROFESSOR HEATHER DIXON-BROWN, 50, director of the CAPE Institute

ANDY DIXON, 35, a vet, brother of Heather

SETTING

The action takes place in three separate locations:

A wildlife rescue centre tucked away in the Cape Otway rainforest. This is also the local veterinary clinic.

A Melbourne CBD apartment.

The office of Professor Dixon-Brown at the CAPE Institute (Conservation and Public Education) in Geelong. The CAPE is a university centre.

All characters and locations are fictitious.

ACT ONE

SCENE ONE

A wildlife rescue centre tucked away in the Cape Otway rainforest. It is a wet and windy night.

An American woman, DR PIPER ROSS, *dressed in khakis (like a park ranger), enters and hurries to her computer.*

The Google homepage appears on the back wall.

PIPER *types in the words 'tiger quoll' and presses Google search. She flicks through various sites that display pictures of the tiger quoll and scrolls down searching for information.*

The sound of a buzzer.

The back wall image clicks off.

PIPER *leaps up and exits, then returns, holding open the door to a man in a heavy rain-jacket, dripping wet.* HARRY JEWELL *enters, cradling an animal wrapped in a towel.*

PIPER: What a night.
HARRY: There's a tree down on the Cape Otway road.
PIPER: May I?

> HARRY *hands her the bundle wrapped in a towel. She carries the bundle to the table.*

Ooh. It's okay. Sssh.
Can you hit the switch? It's just there.
HARRY: This?
PIPER: Yes.

> *The examination table is illuminated.* PIPER *unwraps the animal, making a quick assessment of the damage.*
>
> *Thunder.*

HARRY: You said there were white gums at the top of your drive. You know how many white gums are out there?

PIPER: It's a wild night. Sorry.

She wraps the animal in a blanket.

HARRY: Have you treated one of these before?

PIPER: No. She's my first. We just have to keep her head covered. Make sure she's warm and safe.

HARRY: I thought it was male.

PIPER: [*to the animal*] It's okay, little one. [*To* HARRY] We're just trying to settle her down. Ssh.

She delicately unwraps a section of the blanket and quickly examines the animal.

HARRY: What about all that blood?

PIPER: That's just a cut. It's the internal bleeding we need to worry about. I'll just have a look.

She rolls back the quoll's eyes.

… Oops … hold tight.

HARRY: Sorry.

PIPER: Not a problem. Those gums look pretty pale. Tummy feels alright.

HARRY: Great.

PIPER: She may have a punctured lung …

HARRY: She's not moving.

PIPER: She's had a big shock—

HARRY: That leg. Doesn't look good.

PIPER: It's broken. That's the least of her worries. [*To the quoll*] Ssh ssh. It's okay. You're gonna be okay.

[*To* HARRY] Gloves. Put them on and then I need you to keep her very, very still.

You're doing great.

We're going to keep her very quiet. Hold her head like this.

She demonstrates.

That's good. Nice and gentle. Reassure her.

She puts on a stethoscope and listens to the heartbeat.

The soft sound of the quoll's heartbeat. This underscores the action to the end of the scene.

She's breathing very rapidly.

HARRY: At least she's breathing.
PIPER: She's in shock. How long ago did it happen?
HARRY: An hour. Give or take. About fifteen minutes before I called you. And then I couldn't find the road.

> PIPER *is looking at her wristwatch.*

Are you counting the number of breaths?

> *She nods.*

There used to be lots of tiger quolls round here, when I was a kid. My mother kept a little bloke—just like this—as a pet.
PIPER: Fifteen … twenty … twenty-three.

> PIPER *looks anxious.*

HARRY: What? What does that mean?
PIPER: It means we need to get some fluids into her. Are you alright?
HARRY: Yep.
PIPER: Hold tight.

> PIPER *leaves him holding the quoll. She goes to the cabinet and takes out a syringe and draws up some saline.*

HARRY: Errol, she called him, Errol Flynn.
What's that?
PIPER: Saline. For shock.

> *She works on the quoll.*

I don't think I'm going to be able to get this into a vein.
HARRY: Am I holding her right?
PIPER: Perfect. I'm just going to inject this into the abdominal cavity. That'll be fine. There we go. Ssssh. Sssh. Should bring down her breathing.

> *The tiger quoll cries.*

HARRY: She's in a shitload of pain.
PIPER: Where did it happen?
HARRY: 'Bout thirty k's back. Just as you come into the national park.

> *Thunder.*

Is there something you can give her?
PIPER: I'll just get her breathing under control.

HARRY: For the pain?
PIPER: There is. In a minute.
HARRY: Shit. Don't die. Please don't die.
PIPER: [*gently*] Tell me about Errol Flynn.
HARRY: If it'd been up to us, we would have taken to Errol with a shotgun.
PIPER: [*to the quoll*] Don't you listen to this.
HARRY: Like all the farmers round here, we hated quolls.
PIPER: How come?
HARRY: They'd get into the chicken runs. And that'd be it—just carnage in there ... And we liked shooting stuff, basically.

The quoll cries.

PIPER: What kind of farm?
HARRY: Dairy cattle.
PIPER: I think her breathing is settling a bit ... [*To the quoll*] Ssh. It's okay.
HARRY: So what do we do now?
PIPER: We wait for the vet.
HARRY: You're not the vet?
PIPER: No. I'm just helping out.
HARRY: Where's the vet, then?
PIPER: He's out on a call.
HARRY: [*taking out his phone*] What's his number?
PIPER: He's out of range. He'll be here soon.
HARRY: Shit.
PIPER: I was hoping there might be a baby in the pouch. Sometimes ...
HARRY: Is there?
PIPER: No.
HARRY: Are you sure?
PIPER: [*snapping*] I know what I'm doing!
  Sorry.
  I'm sorry. No-one has seen one of these for a long time. A lot of people around here have given up hope. The last sighting was ten years ago. And that was just a hair in a trap.
HARRY: What do you do, then?
PIPER: I'm a zoologist.
HARRY: Okay.

He strokes the quoll with a tenderness that could break your heart.

PIPER: Most people wouldn't have stopped. Why did you stop?
HARRY: I saw it run out onto the road. I just saw the spots and I thought, shit that's a tiger quoll and then I hit it.

I was speaking on the phone to my daughter. She's fourteen. She rang to let me know that I've destroyed her life.

Pause.

PIPER: Fourteen-year-old girls can be very melodramatic. As I recall.

The quoll cries.

Ssh. Ssh. Come on, girl. [*To* HARRY] You're sopping. You wanna take off your coat?
HARRY: Thanks.

He removes his coat.

More thunder.

PIPER: Would you like a whisky?
HARRY: Most people round here drink tea in a crisis.
PIPER: I'm not from round here.

She holds up the whisky bottle.

HARRY: American?

He pours two glasses.

PIPER: Michigan. Originally.
HARRY: Nice.
PIPER: You been there?
HARRY: Years ago. I did postgrad at Columbia.

Beat.

My wife is having 'sexual relations' with my friend Damien Gore. That's what I wanted to scream down the phone to my daughter. I'm not the one who destroyed this marriage. Ask your mother what it's like going down on Damien-fucking-Gore.

But you can't say that to a fourteen-year-old girl.
PIPER: Best not!
HARRY: According to my wife, it's all my fault.
PIPER: Wow.

HARRY: Sorry, I'm blathering. What's he doing, this vet?
PIPER: He's pulling out a calf.
HARRY: Okay.
PIPER: It's dead. He has to chop it up and pull it out piece by piece. It's been dead for three days.
HARRY: Yeah. Gross. Poor guy.
  Can you phone him and tell him this is a bloody tiger quoll?
PIPER: He's going as fast as he can.
HARRY: Look. I don't want to be responsible for killing the last one of these things.
PIPER: If there's one, there'll be more.
HARRY: How do you know? Maybe this is the last one. There is always a last one, isn't there? The last thylacine. The last dodo. Maybe this is the last tiger quoll.
  So … maybe this makes room for something new.
PIPER: More cats. That's all it makes room for.
HARRY: So cats replace quolls. That's what evolution's all about, isn't it? Natural selection.
PIPER: But it's not natural. It's unnatural. Millions of tiny relationships hang off the fangs of the quoll. And when those relationships break apart—
HARRY: What are you doing here? In the bush on your own.
PIPER: I'm a volunteer. I work at the university.
  At the Institute for Conservation and Public Education. The CAPE Institute. In Geelong.
HARRY: I'm impressed.
PIPER: You know it?
HARRY: Never heard of it.
  So what do you do at this CAPE Institute?
PIPER: I do koalas.
HARRY: I thought I'd seen you somewhere. You were in the paper a few weekends back.
PIPER: I'm on leave from the San Diego Zoo. We have the biggest koala breeding program outside of Australia.
HARRY: That's right. You're the koala girl.
PIPER: Do you know that female koalas choose their mate by smell?
HARRY: Really? That's very intimate.

PIPER: I've been taking samples from the scent glands of male koalas. And pretty soon I'll be able to create an artificial scent, like a male cologne which will trick girl koalas into falling in love with a better type of boy.
HARRY: Really? So what will it smell like, your perfume?
PIPER: It's a very sexy combination of urine and faeces.
HARRY: So, just a dab.

PIPER laughs.

The sound of tyres on gravel outside.

PIPER: Here he is.
What happened to Errol Flynn, by the way?
HARRY: One night he didn't show up and we never saw him again. My mum said he'd found a good woman.
PIPER: Not likely. They're party boys. As soon as their gonads fire up, they go crazy and have as much sex as they can. Then they collapse and die!
HARRY: I could think of worse ways to leave the building.

ANDY enters.

PIPER: Andy!
ANDY: G'day. How'd you go?
PIPER: We're hanging on. Only just.
ANDY: Sorry, I stink.
Is it a quoll?
PIPER: Mm hm.

ANDY walks directly to the table.

ANDY: She's a tiger, alright. What happened?
HARRY: I hit her on the road.
ANDY: Obviously.
PIPER: Andy, this is … Sorry, I don't even know your name.
HARRY: Harry.
PIPER: Harry.
ANDY: G'day.

ANDY checks the quoll, expertly.

PIPER: Her lungs sound terrible. I thought maybe she had a diaphragmatic hernia.

ANDY: Why would you think that?

Beat.

PIPER: The diaphragm feels as though it's separated and shooting forward ...

ANDY: You reckon?

He continues examining the quoll.

Did you check the pulse?

PIPER: Of course I checked the pulse.

ANDY: And?

PIPER: Sounds okay.

ANDY: What about refill?

PIPER: I checked the gums. And the eyes.

ANDY looks unimpressed.

I didn't want to stress her any more than necessary.

ANDY checks the animal in silence.

I did everything I could.

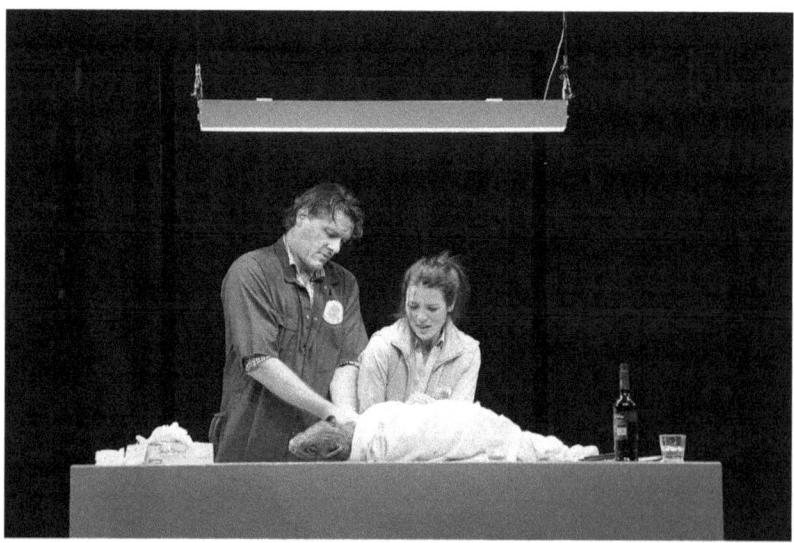

Myles Pollard as Andy and Hannah Day as Piper in Black Swan State Theatre Company's 2015 production of EXTINCTION. *(Photo: Gary Marsh)*

Beat.

ANDY: Where did it happen?
HARRY: I'm not sure exactly.
ANDY: You'll have a GPS in that car, I'm assuming?
HARRY: Yeah. D'you want me to check it out?

ANDY nods cursorily.

HARRY exits.

PIPER: What is your problem?
ANDY: I don't have a problem.

ANDY holds up the whisky bottle, accusingly.

PIPER: The guy is upset. He's had an accident.
ANDY: Hope he didn't damage that cruise missile he's got out there.
PIPER: You're judging the guy by the type of car he drives?
ANDY: Why d'you think blokes like him buy wheels like that?
PIPER: Andy! The guy hit an animal and he stopped.

Thunder.

On a night like this.
ANDY: Come here.
PIPER: Why?
ANDY: Just come over here.
PIPER: No. You totally undermined me, in front of him.
ANDY: Piper. I'm cold. I'm tired. And I've had my arm up the arse end of a cow for the past three hours. Now if you come here I will show you what you needed to feel for. The quoll has a broken back. It's paralysed from the waist down. It's not fair to try and resuscitate an animal in this condition.

HARRY re-enters, dripping wet. He holds up his phone.

HARRY: Wild Dog Creek Road.
    Just before the old Colac turnoff.
ANDY: From around here, are you?
HARRY: Used to be.

ANDY takes a large syringe. He draws up a substance into it.

PIPER: What are you doing?

ANDY: She can't survive these injuries.
PIPER: Andy!? What are you doing? Andy?

> *He euthanises the quoll. It dies.*
>
> *The heartbeat stops. Silence.*

ANDY: Do you want your towel?

> HARRY *stares coldly at* ANDY *while he wraps the animal up and puts it in a box and seals it.*

PIPER: I don't believe you just did that.
HARRY: This was not somebody's mangy cat, you know.
ANDY: Really?
HARRY: You don't just pull out your needle and dispose of the problem.
PIPER: We needed to at least *try*.
ANDY: You snapped its spinal column.
HARRY: You do what you can to keep an endangered animal alive.
ANDY: Not if it's paralysed, you don't!
HARRY: Yes, you do! Unless you're the village idiot posing as the fucking vet.

> HARRY *picks up his coat and heads for the door.*

ANDY: Nice meeting you too, mate.

> PIPER *follows* HARRY *to the door.*

PIPER: I'm so sorry. I don't know what to say.

> HARRY *fishes for his card. He gives it to* PIPER.

HARRY: Call me.
PIPER: I'm Piper.
HARRY: I figured that.
PIPER: Thank you. For what you did.

> HARRY *is about to leave, but turns back.*

HARRY: Is there somewhere I can read about your koala project?

> PIPER *gives him her card.*

PIPER: That's my website.

> HARRY *leaves his card on the desk and exits.*

  Oh. He's left his phone. Harry?

She runs out after him.

ANDY *begins to tidy up. He pours himself a whisky, keeping an eye on* PIPER *and* HARRY *outside.*

Eventually the car starts up and we hear tyres on gravel as HARRY *drives away.*

PIPER *re-enters. She collects her motorcycle helmet and her pack.*

ANDY: What are you doing?
PIPER: What's it look like?
ANDY: Piper? I had no choice.
PIPER: You did so. You just opted for the most convenient one.

She exits.

ANDY *examines Harry's business card. He leaps up, brandishing it in the air.*

ANDY: [*calling*] You know who this dude is?! Piper?! Piper?! It's Harry Jewell! Piper?! It's Harry bloody Jewell!

The roar of a motorbike.

ANDY *becomes unsteady on his feet and falls to the floor.*

SCENE TWO

The small balcony of an apartment looking across at a sea of other apartments in the centre of the city. This is the home of Professor Heather Dixon-Brown.

She is reading messages on her phone and consulting papers in her briefcase. It is early evening. The noise of the city and peak-hour traffic rumbles below.

DIXON-BROWN: [*calling*] No ice with mine!

PIPER *enters, carrying drinks.*

PIPER: Happy birthday!
DIXON-BROWN: What's this?
PIPER: Watermelon tequila.
DIXON-BROWN: [*sipping*] Oh, my God.
PIPER: Nice?

DIXON-BROWN: *Oh, my God!*
Did I tell you I had a meeting with the vice-chancellor today? Apparently we're at war. I swear to God, he leaned across the table and started to talk to me urgently about defending our territory. It was like we were in the White House Situation Room.
PIPER: Who's the enemy?
DIXON-BROWN: Other universities.
PIPER: Right.
DIXON-BROWN: He wants to 're-brand' us. As 'Harvard Down Under'.
PIPER: Wow.
DIXON-BROWN: *What is* in this drink?
PIPER: Just watermelon, all mushed up with ice, sugar syrup, blueberries and tequila. My mom used to make it for her bridge nights.
DIXON-BROWN: How is your mum?
PIPER: She's on a hunger strike.

Pause.

DIXON-BROWN: Meaning ... like a diet?
PIPER: Meaning like Gandhi. Like non-violent resistance. The Dean of her university is amalgamating her beloved Philosophy department with Cinema Studies.
DIXON-BROWN: And I thought we were insane.
Good for her.

She toasts PIPER *with her own delicious tequila mush.*

To Alison.
PIPER: People who have normal mothers don't understand the horrors of having a weird one.
Yours is totally ... sane ... She makes soup and knits you jumpers. Mine is like this mad, moulting hen.
She dashes around the country promoting veganism, but do you know what she actually eats?
Corn chips. That is all there is standing between Alison and malnutrition.

PIPER *refills her glass.*

DIXON-BROWN: We have to talk about what you're going to do.
PIPER: About what?

DIXON-BROWN: Your funding here runs out in three months. You either have to go back to San Diego, or we find you a new project.
PIPER: What sort of project?
DIXON-BROWN: I had a meeting with the Environment Minister this morning.
　　She wants me to update the Dixon-Brown Index and include birds.
PIPER: [*finding this awkward territory*] Oh, Dix ... the index.
DIXON-BROWN: What?
PIPER: When would this be?
DIXON-BROWN: Next month.
PIPER: Oh, no. I can't. I'm sorry. We're collecting scent samples from my koalas on Phillip Island.
DIXON-BROWN: Piper—
PIPER: I need this data. My whole project depends on it.
DIXON-BROWN: But you don't have to collect the samples yourself.
PIPER: I do.
DIXON-BROWN: You have money for a research assistant.
PIPER: I know.
DIXON-BROWN: You have to learn to delegate.
PIPER: I know. I just don't think you can be an ecologist from a desk in the Jean Prouse Building.

　　Beat.

DIXON-BROWN: [*coolly*] I run the institute. I don't have the luxury of spending months at a time in the bush.
PIPER: I didn't mean you.
DIXON-BROWN: I would love nothing more than to get back to my own research.
PIPER: I know, I'm sorry, I'm talking about myself and the index—
DIXON-BROWN: I look at Stuart Decker and I think, 'How come you get to spend six months collecting coral from the Great Barrier Reef?' Oh, that's right. Some mug spends all her time in her dingy little office writing your applications so you can win the Humboldt Award and get a suntan.
PIPER: [*looking out at the city skyline*] You live up here and you never even see a bird.

　　DIXON-BROWN *pours herself another glass.*

No wonder you're stressed.
DIXON-BROWN: I'm not stressed!
PIPER: But how do you renew yourself—if you never see a flock of birds sail across the sky in the morning light?
DIXON-BROWN: You drink.
PIPER: You can't experience awe in a city.
DIXON-BROWN: That is ridiculous.
PIPER: It's not. You have to be in the wilderness to feel reverence. You have to be someplace where life is unfolding *beyond* human control.
   Why don't you come with me into the bush, just for a couple of days? That'll sort you out.
DIXON-BROWN: Piper! I'm not the one who needs to be sorted out.
PIPER: I know zip about birds.
DIXON-BROWN: They fly in flocks across the sky in the morning light.
   Look, the question is, do you want to stay or not?
PIPER: I want to stay. You know I do.

The muffled sound of ANDY*'s voice.*

DIXON-BROWN *talks into the intercom.*

DIXON-BROWN: Hiya. Come on up.
PIPER: Is that Andy? What's he doing here?
DIXON-BROWN: It's my birthday. He's my brother.
PIPER: I'm outta here.
DIXON-BROWN: Please, Pipe. Mum and Dad will be at the restaurant too. They adore you.
PIPER: Andy and I aren't speaking.
DIXON-BROWN: Jesus, Piper.
   The tiger quoll had a broken back.
PIPER: It may have had a chance. Maybe it was just a damaged vertebra. How do we know?
DIXON-BROWN: He's a vet.
PIPER: He's not God.
DIXON-BROWN: Remember when the two of you rode that motorbike across the Simpson Desert?
PIPER: What about it?
DIXON-BROWN: You should have been married to Nigel. His idea of

extreme adventure was buying his socks from a different department store.

Beat.

He sent through the divorce papers.

PIPER: No wonder you're depressed.

DIXON-BROWN: I am *not* depressed. What is it with you? I'm just over being single. But I have no room in my life for a relationship. There is no empty space that is boyfriend-shaped.

Pause.

PIPER: You have to create the space—

DIXON-BROWN: There are twenty-five people on staff at the institute— most of whom have families and mortgages and they rely on me to come up with their salaries. So, as much as I would love to be out there in the bush or cruising bars looking for a bloke, I just can't.

She sighs.

PIPER: Cruising bars?

DIXON-BROWN: Whatever.

    PIPER *giggles.*

Ther sound of the intercom buzzer.

ANDY: [*offstage*] Hey, Sis.

DIXON-BROWN: Come for dinner. Please?

Before waiting for an answer, DIXON-BROWN *opens the door. It is* ANDY. *He kisses his sister. He is sporting a cut across his forehead and a black eye.*

ANDY: Happy birthday!

He hands her a present.

DIXON-BROWN: What happened to you?

ANDY: Hey, Pipes.

PIPER: Omigod.

ANDY: I had an altercation with a door.

DIXON-BROWN: Whereabouts?

ANDY: At bloody Pascoe's. [*By way of explanation to* DIXON-BROWN] This massive dairy farm, out at Ryler's Ridge.

DIXON-BROWN: That looks as if it needs a stitch. Come here.
ANDY: She'll be right.
DIXON-BROWN: Let me look.
ANDY: What's this?
PIPER: Watermelon tequila. Want some?
ANDY: Sure. [*Fending off his sister*] It's okay.

> DIXON-BROWN *represses the desire to fuss.*

DIXON-BROWN: I'll get you a glass.

> *She exits.*

ANDY: I'm sorry.
PIPER: Have you seen a doctor?
ANDY: Yeah, it's fine.
PIPER: You haven't, have you?

> ANDY *grabs her arm, whispering to her urgently before* DIXON-BROWN *gets back.*

ANDY: I hate it when we fight.
PIPER: Well, stop arguing with me all the time.
ANDY: I didn't start it.
PIPER: You did.
ANDY: I didn't. You got into a big sulk and left.
PIPER: Andy, I am not the kind of person who sulks.

> *Beat.*

Alright. Sulking is part of my repertoire. But that was not a sulk. That was like fury.
ANDY: You're so sexy when you're furious.
PIPER: There has not been a confirmed sighting of a tiger quoll for ten years.

> ANDY *remembers something.*

ANDY: Oh, by the way, your Mr Jewell is in the news.
PIPER: Who?
ANDY: Your Harry Jewell. He's the Managing Director of Powerhouse Mining.
PIPER: No!
ANDY: Your Mr Evil.

PIPER: He's not *my* Mr Evil.

ANDY: He's applied for a license to explore for brown coal. In the Otways …

PIPER: You're joking.

ANDY: Eighty thousand hectares of prime agricultural land.

PIPER: The government won't let him.

ANDY: You just watch 'em.

PIPER: What is the matter with these people! Are you sure it's the same Harry Jewell?

> ANDY *consults his phone. He types.*

ANDY: J. E. W. E. Double-L.

'Mr Jewell founded Powerhouse last year, after two decades' experience in the coal and gold sectors.'

[*Summarising*] Holds a Masters degree in Mining Engineering from Columbia University in New York. Married with one daughter.

PIPER: That's my Mr Evil.

> ANDY *is scrolling down through his emails.*

ANDY: The locals are furious. Here's an email from Corkie Dent. 'If any bastard tries to shift any of my dirt, looking for coal, I'll blow his arse off.'

> PIPER *laughs.*

PIPER: Good ol' Corkie.

> ANDY *draws her to him and kisses her passionately.*

> DIXON-BROWN *enters, then does a double-take and exits.*

ANDY: Dix!

Come and open your present.

PIPER: You and I need to sort out some things, Andy.

ANDY: [*flirting*] I like it when we sort things out.

PIPER: [*flirting*] Do you just?

ANDY: I do.

> DIXON-BROWN *enters again just as* ANDY *is scooping* PIPER *toward him.*

DIXON-BROWN: Oh, purlease.

ANDY: Dix! Here.

He hands DIXON-BROWN *a little box left on the table.*

DIXON-BROWN: This doesn't look like a book about climate change.

ANDY *grins.*

DIXON-BROWN *holds up a very pretty necklace.*

Did you choose this?
ANDY: I did.
DIXON-BROWN: Andy, it's beautiful.
ANDY: Here.

He fiddles with the clasp and attaches the necklace around her neck.

PIPER: That's lovely.
ANDY: Mm. You have a very nice … thorax …
DIXON-BROWN: Excuse me, did you just pay me a compliment?
ANDY: Cheers!

He takes a sip.

You should see this dairy farm. It's all computerised. They've got one bloke managing a thousand cows. No human supervision of the milking. No-one to check the udders. I'm just there, doing the rounds. Like a robot.
DIXON-BROWN: It's work, I suppose.
ANDY: That's not why I became a vet.
DIXON-BROWN: Is that when you hit your head?
ANDY: That's when I thought, 'I'm going to sell the practice'.
DIXON-BROWN: Sell the practice?
PIPER: And do what?
ANDY: Maybe go back to El Salvador. Or Zambia. Somewhere where it means something to be a vet.
DIXON-BROWN: What about Piper?
ANDY: Piper's leaving.
DIXON-BROWN: No, she's not.
ANDY: [*to* PIPER] What?
DIXON-BROWN: She's going to work on updating the Dixon-Brown Index with me.
PIPER: Oh, Dix. I don't think so.
DIXON-BROWN: Why not?

PIPER: You need someone who's good at math.
DIXON-BROWN: That would be me. I have a PhD in Statistics. In case I forgot to mention it.
PIPER: Being such a self-effacing person.
DIXON-BROWN: Being such a fucking *doormat*.
PIPER: For Stuart-fucking-Decker.
DIXON-BROWN: And every other fucking *fucker* in this department.
I love this drink. Is there more?
PIPER: Sure.
ANDY: How much tequila is in this?
PIPER: A shitload.
DIXON-BROWN: I better have some more, then.

> PIPER *re-fills her glass from a jug.*

What is your problem, Piper?
ANDY: Her problem is that she would no more work on your fucking index, than fly to the moon.
PIPER: Andy!
DIXON-BROWN: I am assuming that you both agree that the rate of extinction is out of control.
PIPER: Of course we do.
DIXON-BROWN: And there is only so much funding to go around to deal with this.

> *Beat.*

You do accept that?

> *Beat.*

Piper! People with expertise—people like you and me—have to be able to advise government about the best use of the conservation dollar.
PIPER: I know the argument.
DIXON-BROWN: We need an objective measure that allows us to say which species are worth saving and which are beyond the point of no return.
PIPER: That's not our call. They are all 'worth saving'.
DIXON-BROWN: But we don't have the money to save them all!
ANDY: So what's your latest magic number?

DIXON-BROWN: Five thousand. Populations below that can't survive a catastrophe like a flood or a cyclone or a bushfire.

ANDY: I thought it was two thousand.

DIXON-BROWN: I've refined the algorithm.

PIPER: And this is supposed to apply to every mammal on earth. That's what your 'algorithm' says. Regardless of whether we are talking about killer whales or teeny potoroos.

DIXON-BROWN: Government departments need a strategy that will deliver the highest probability of success.

PIPER: So now we're doing birds. Which means consigning the orange-bellied parrot to the trash!

DIXON-BROWN: Probably.

ANDY: There are only twenty-one left.

DIXON-BROWN: Functionally extinct.

PIPER: This is assassination by numbers.

DIXON-BROWN: This is living in the real world.

PIPER: This is signing the death warrant.

ANDY: See what I have to put up with?

PIPER & DIXON-BROWN: [*together*] Shut up.

PIPER: What about the tiger quoll? Are you prepared to say, 'There's a species that's done for'?

DIXON-BROWN: Probably. The quoll you treated the other night—

PIPER: The quoll *your brother* killed.

DIXON-BROWN: The quoll *my brother* killed—

ANDY: The quoll your brother *humanely euthanised* had no chance of surviving through the night.

PIPER: You know what I think? Your index is a calculus of death.

DIXON-BROWN: Nice.

ANDY: Punchy.

DIXON-BROWN: But not, I think, a line we'll be using on the website. Are you going to wear that [*park ranger outfit with shorts*] to the restaurant?

PIPER: Have you got a change of socks?

DIXON-BROWN: Go grab something from my wardrobe.

PIPER: Like a suit or something?

DIXON-BROWN: You can wear a ball gown if you want.

PIPER: Andy?

ANDY: You look beautiful just as you are.
DIXON-BROWN: We're going to the Florentino.
PIPER: They have a no-shorts policy?
DIXON-BROWN: It's my birthday. No shorts.
PIPER: Have I got time for a shower?
ANDY: No.
PIPER: I can't go if I don't shower.
DIXON-BROWN: Piper!

    PIPER *exits.*

    ANDY *polishes off the remaining watermelon tequila.*

Can you please find me a man to marry? I want to be a housewife.
ANDY: I told you. I found you a man.
DIXON-BROWN: What man?
ANDY: Alan Dodd. Recently divorced. Teaches meditation part-time. Works in IT.
DIXON-BROWN: You know what Nigel used to say to me? 'You're one of those women who looks better with your clothes on.' What sort of a man says that?

    ANDY *picks up an invoice on* DIXON-BROWN'*s desk.*

ANDY: What's this?
DIXON-BROWN: Excuse me?

    She tries to take it off him, but he won't let her.

ANDY: Full leg and bikini: forty-five dollars; lip and chin: twenty; underarm: fifteen; eyebrow— Do you have your eyebrows *sculpted*?
DIXON-BROWN: Give it to me, Andy.
ANDY: Two hundred and sixty-seven dollars.
DIXON-BROWN: That's for a haircut as well.
ANDY: How often do you get this done?
DIXON-BROWN: Every five weeks.
ANDY: Every five weeks, you spend two hundred and sixty-seven dollars on hair removal?
    You could get a tree lopped for that.
DIXON-BROWN: What's he look like—this Alan Dodd? If he's in IT, he's probably overweight, lives with his mother. Shy to the point of autism.
ANDY: Dix.

DIXON-BROWN: What?

> *Beat.*

ANDY: I fell over last night.
DIXON-BROWN: Andy.
ANDY: I just walked into the house and fell down.
DIXON-BROWN: W—what's this about?
ANDY: [*with a shrug*] That hasn't happened before.
DIXON-BROWN: Did you see a doctor?
ANDY: Tomorrow.
DIXON-BROWN: Andy!
ANDY: I think this might be the start.

> *Beat.*

DIXON-BROWN: You have to tell her.
ANDY: No.
DIXON-BROWN: Andy! You have to.
ANDY: Dix, you know what she's like. She'll stay up all night looking after a bloody possum.
DIXON-BROWN: So?
ANDY: So. She'll want children. I'm not going to ask her to waste her life. I'm not doing that.

SCENE THREE

The animal shelter.

PIPER *is Skyping with her mother. She is talking on a headset with a built-in mic. The computer-camera is on the desk. She is also carrying a possum around in a papoose.*

PIPER: Mom, I am not being passive aggressive. I am just trying—

> …
> What?
> …
> It's a possum.
> …
> No, it is not a baby substitute.
> …
> Andy. I'm at his place.

…
   [*To* ANDY] Hello, Andy.
ANDY: Hello, Alison.
PIPER: [*to Skype*] Hello, Alison.
   …
   Hang on …
   ANDY *is leaving.*
[*To* ANDY] When are you back?
ANDY: I've got an appointment up in town.
PIPER: For work?
ANDY: No.
PIPER: What?
   He gives her a mind-your-own-business look.
Andy?
[*To Skype*] Hang on, Mom—
   …
   What?
   …
   [*To* ANDY] She wants to speak to you.
   ANDY *indicates he doesn't want to.*
[*To Skype*] He's in a hurry.
   …
   ANDY *is annoyed.*
What's this about, Mom? He's racing out the door.
   …
   [*To* ANDY] Andy, please. She just needs a minute.
   ANDY *takes the headphones off* PIPER, *irritated. He then sits in front of the computer transformed into a smiling, calm and sweet man.*
ANDY: Hey. Alison. How's it going, mate?
   …
   Oh. Shit.
   …
   Oh.

...
 Oh, no.
PIPER: What?
ANDY: Oh, that's no good.
PIPER: What's going on? Andy?
ANDY: [*to* PIPER] Beast is sick.
PIPER: Beast? What's the matter with Beast?
ANDY: Ssh.
PIPER: Tell me! Tell me!
ANDY: [*to Skype*] Hold on, Alison. Piper's losing it, here. [*To* PIPER] He's got cancer.
PIPER: Cancer. Beast has got cancer? What kind of cancer? How does she know? Put her on. Has she taken him to the—?
ANDY: Yes. Calm down.
PIPER: Put her on. Don't tell me to calm down.
ANDY: Let me just get the facts.
PIPER: Why didn't she tell me?
 Pause.
ANDY: [*to Skype*] Right. Okay.
PIPER: What?
ANDY: [*to* PIPER] He has a tumour on the lung.
PIPER: Can they operate?
ANDY: Hang on. [*To Skype*] Sorry, Alison. What was that?
...
 'Course. And that's what they said? You've seen this guy before?
PIPER: Dr Kurtz. Is it Dr Kurtz?
ANDY: [*to* PIPER] No. They have a specialist oncology unit.
 [*To Skype, for* PIPER*'s information*] They can operate to remove the tumour and then do a course of radiation.
...
PIPER: Andy?
ANDY: That sounds about right. But once you factor in the CT scans, the surgery and follow-up therapy—
PIPER: He's my dog!
ANDY: Alison, I think Piper needs to speak to you.
 ...
 Yes.

...
Of course. I understand.
...
Mm hm.
...
I'll put her on.

PIPER *grabs the headphones.*

PIPER: [*to Skype*] Why didn't you tell me? You sat on the phone and you didn't say a word.
...
I just knew something like this would happen. You don't care about animals. You have no idea about how to care for anyone. You can't even look after yourself. I should never, *ever* have left him with you.

ANDY: Piper, come on. [*To Skype*] Alison. We'll call you back, okay?

He pulls the headset lead out.

Alright. Calm down.
PIPER: I'll raise the money, Andy.
ANDY: Yep.
PIPER: I'll sell my bike.
ANDY: Mm hm.
PIPER: How much is it going to cost?
ANDY: Fifteen, twenty thousand.
PIPER: This is so not fair.
ANDY: Beast is an old dog, Pipe.
PIPER: Nn nn. You don't understand.
ANDY: I do.
PIPER: He understands me more than anyone in the world.
ANDY: Thanks.
PIPER: I should never have left him with *her*.
ANDY: This is not her fault, Pipe.

PIPER *paces.*

PIPER: Will his hair fall out?
ANDY: We're not going down that path.
PIPER: What do you mean? I'm talking about chemotherapy.
ANDY: Animals get sick. And they die.

PIPER: Not Beast.
ANDY: Even Beast.
PIPER: No. I'm not ready.
ANDY: Piper, remember when Bryan took Twinkie in for a pacemaker?
PIPER: That was different.
ANDY: You were scathing!
PIPER: Beast is a person. He's like a brother.
ANDY: And Alison treats him like a son. She *paid* for him to have a hip replacement, remember? [*Incredulously*] She takes him to Central Park every day and feeds him cubes of fruit salad from a plastic fork at that café.
PIPER: You don't understand New Yorkers.
ANDY: Piper. Listen to me.
PIPER: If you loved someone and they were dying, you would do everything you could to help them.

She buries her head into the possum and sobs.

ANDY *is about to hug her when the bell dings for reception. He exits.*

PIPER *talks to the possum.*

You'd do everything you could, wouldn't you? Because life is precious, isn't it, you poor little thing.

ANDY *re-enters.*

ANDY: It's Mr Evil.
PIPER: What's he want?
ANDY: [*with a shrug*] He wants to have sex with you.
PIPER: He does not.
ANDY: His wife has just left him.
PIPER: You have such a rudimentary understanding of human psychology.
ANDY: Some people aren't that complicated.
PIPER: Tell him to piss off.
ANDY: Okay. Listen, babe, I have to get to Melbourne. Shit. It's nine o'clock.
   Are you gonna be okay?

PIPER *nods.*

ANDY: You need to call Alison back.

PIPER: Why?
ANDY: She drove from New York to San Diego to collect Beast. To look after him for you.
PIPER: I am not gonna apologise.
ANDY: You sure about that?
PIPER: Of course I'm sure.
ANDY: Okay.

He kisses her.

PIPER: Andy, can you … deal with him?
ANDY: Will you be here tonight?

She shrugs.

Okay. Give us a call, later.

He leaves.

PIPER *puts the possum back in its cage.*

She busies herself putting things away and collecting her stuff. When she looks up, HARRY *is waving to her at the window.*

HARRY: Sorry about your dog.
PIPER: What are you doing?
HARRY: I need to talk to you.

PIPER *lets him in.*

PIPER: You're going to get lynched.
HARRY: Who's going to lynch me?
PIPER: I am. With a few thousand other people in this community.
    You didn't happen to mention the other night that you're a coalminer.
HARRY: It didn't come up.
PIPER: No, it didn't. Interesting, that.
HARRY: What's the matter with your dog?
PIPER: He has a tumour on his lung.

HARRY *sees she is about to cry.*

HARRY: They can treat that. How old is he?
PIPER: Twelve.
HARRY: Whatever they can do on humans, they can do on dogs.

PIPER: If you've got a spare fifteen thousand dollars.
HARRY: Fifteen grand. Come on. This is your best friend we're talking about.

> PIPER *starts to cry.*

What sort of dog?
PIPER: American water spaniel. He was a rescue dog. I got him when he was six weeks old.

> *She pulls herself together.*

You had me convinced you were someone who cared about the environment.
HARRY: Actually, it's the *word* I really don't care for. 'The environment'. Mostly because it's associated with *environmentalists*.
PIPER: We're not the ones turning this country into a big empty hole.
HARRY. Not true. We fill in our holes. It's called 'rehabilitation'. We are required by law to do it!
PIPER: After you've caused massive damage to the ecosystem.
HARRY: Look—I'm not a hero, Piper. I don't want to talk about this.
PIPER: I'm sure you don't.
HARRY: I can't save the world, okay? But I *can* help to bring jobs and people back to my home town.
PIPER: We don't want your jobs.
HARRY: Who's this '*we*'? You don't serve your cause by being indifferent to the interests of working people.

> *Beat.*

Anyway, show me something else that'll turn the lights on.
PIPER: Solar. Wind. Tide.
HARRY: Yeah. Tell the Chinese. They'll go on buying coal wherever they can get it, because the lights don't go out when the sun goes down.
PIPER: Blame the Chinese. Good work.
HARRY: They have a right to electricity.
    Piper, can we talk about the other night?
PIPER: What about it?
HARRY: I know you feel hostile towards me. But can you just hear me out? I had hoped we could talk about setting up a project to save the Otway quolls.

PIPER: What sort of a project?
HARRY: Getting rid of the cats for a start. Then you tell me. How do we find the tiger quolls? What do we need to do, to fix up that forest? You're the one with the know-how, Piper. I'm just the investor.
PIPER: What sort of investment?
HARRY: You mean how much money? [*He shrugs.*] Whatever it takes.

Beat.

I spent yesterday with my mother.

Beat.

She was impressed that an American might devote herself to our koalas. We saw about six of them. In the manna gums on the lighthouse road. We also saw crimson rosellas. Heaps of them. Mum goes, 'I've been unfaithful to your father. I keep falling in love with birds.'

PIPER *softens a fraction.*

PIPER: How did she take your news? Your separation?
HARRY: On the chin. Like she takes everything.
PIPER: She didn't side with your wife?
HARRY: No, actually she was quite loving.

Beat.

Listen. I'm on my way to Kangaroo Island. You been there?
PIPER: No.
HARRY: You have to see this place. It's a wildlife paradise. Totally pristine. They don't have foxes or rabbits. No feral cats, so the bush is teeming with birds. Goannas. Wallabies. You name it. Bone-white beaches with sea lions flopping about. It's the kind of place where people make their own cheese and honey. Farmers advertise for wives on community noticeboards.
PIPER: Is that why you're going?
HARRY: I'm not in the market for a wife.

Beat.

Why don't you come?
PIPER: Now?
HARRY: I've chartered a plane. There's a bloke at the airport waiting for my call.

PIPER: No carbon footprint too great for such important work.
   I have to work this weekend.
HARRY: Really? I can't tempt you to fly along the coastline, over the Twelve Apostles—following the line of the Great Southern Ocean? Then along the Limestone Coast. Over the Coorong? Only take a couple of hours. Ever been to any of these places?
PIPER: No.
HARRY: Piper!
PIPER: Life is long.

> HARRY *smiles.*

HARRY: That's why I like you.
PIPER: You don't know me.
HARRY: I don't get to meet people like you very often.
PIPER: What kind of people do you get to meet?
HARRY: Dickheads mostly.
PIPER: No-one around here wants a coalmine, Harry.
HARRY: No-one will touch the forest. I'm looking at an area about sixty k's west of here.
PIPER: Why are you going to Kangaroo Island?
HARRY: So I can show you one of the most beautiful places on earth.
PIPER: You don't give up, do you?
HARRY: Never.
PIPER: I'm in a relationship.
HARRY: No worries. You'll be home in time for dinner.
PIPER: I've always wanted to see the Coorong.
HARRY: Get your stuff then.
PIPER: No.

SCENE FOUR

Dixon-Brown's apartment.

It is very late. Maybe three a.m. DIXON-BROWN, *in her nightgown, opens the door to* ANDY.

ANDY: I'm drunk.
DIXON-BROWN: Is that right?
ANDY: Can I stay?

DIXON-BROWN: That depends. Are you going to vomit?
ANDY: Probably.
DIXON-BROWN: Where have you been?
ANDY: Bar 66.
DIXON-BROWN: That's a gay bar.
ANDY: Yeah.
DIXON-BROWN: You've turned gay?
ANDY: I need to lie down in that room in there.
DIXON-BROWN: Not in there. Not on my sheets. [*Indicating the sofa*] You can lie down here.
ANDY: Could you turn the ceiling off?
DIXON-BROWN: Oh, Andy.
ANDY: I went with Mickey Chin.
DIXON-BROWN: Is he gay?
ANDY: No.
DIXON-BROWN: You want water?
ANDY: No-one tried to pick me up.
DIXON-BROWN: Disappointing.
ANDY: Why do you think that is?
DIXON-BROWN: Maybe because you're a screaming heterosexual.
ANDY: Is it that obvious?
DIXON-BROWN: Here.

She hands him water and pills, and watches him take them.

What did the doctor say?
ANDY: Oh, the doctor.
DIXON-BROWN: Andy?
ANDY: He told me my life is over. No, that's not true. I asked him how I could *make* it over, but he wouldn't play ball on that one. Even when I said to him, people bring their dogs to me and I put them down. Because that's the loving thing to do. That's the caring, humane course of action, Doctor Wynn. But he told me we had a long way to go before we got to that stage of the game.
DIXON-BROWN: How long?
ANDY: Oh, anything up to five years. Which is a long time. In dog years.
DIXON-BROWN: I wish I'd come with you.
ANDY: No, you don't.

DIXON-BROWN: Did you tell him about Grandpa?
ANDY: Of course I told him about Grandpa.
DIXON-BROWN: Told him what?
ANDY: The facts. That by the time Grandpa was my age, he'd lost all muscle co-ordination. He trembled. And then he went blind. Then he lost the ability to speak. And after a few more years he went mad. And still, there is no treatment.

Silence.

This is the reason I don't tell Piper.
DIXON-BROWN: Did you tell Mickey Chin?
ANDY: No. Why would I tell Mickey Chin?
DIXON-BROWN: He's your friend, isn't he?
ANDY: There is nothing anyone can say, Heather. Nothing. Not even *you* can think of anything to say.

You just stand there. And to be perfectly frank, that makes it worse.
DIXON-BROWN: I'm sorry. I just want to be there for you, Andy.
ANDY: You assume that this will help me bear the burden. Is that right? This public announcement you're hell-bent on me making.
DIXON-BROWN: Not a public announcement.
ANDY: A private confession then.
DIXON-BROWN: I just think it would help to tell your friends.
ANDY: Help who? You think it will help *me*?
DIXON-BROWN: Yes. I think it will help *you*.
ANDY: Well, it won't. It will not lighten the burden. It will make the burden worse. It will make the burden heavier and harder. I have to lug around the weight of another person's misery in addition to my own.
DIXON-BROWN: I'm sorry, Andy. I really am.
ANDY: I'm sure you're sorry. I'm sorry as well. And everyone who eventually learns about my illness will be very sorry too. We'll all be sorry. So *terribly* sorry.
DIXON-BROWN: I wish I could be better.
ANDY: What an asinine thing to say—better than what?!
DIXON-BROWN: More comforting.
ANDY: Yeah, it's all going to work out in the end. Fuck. Off.
DIXON-BROWN: Okay.
ANDY: See, this kind of conversation just brings out the *idiot* in people.

And to think that the very person you're closest to could be so grotesquely inept at helping you—that's actually a reason for despair.

DIXON-BROWN: Maybe we should talk about this in the morning. When you feel better.

ANDY: I'm never gonna feel better. The gun's gone off, Heather. And I'm running as fast as I can towards blindness and gibbering dementia. I am never going to feel better. Do you hear me?

DIXON-BROWN: Yes.

ANDY: Can you understand what it means?

DIXON-BROWN: No. I can't really.

ANDY: Good. Good. Now we're getting somewhere.

> ANDY *has made his point. He exits.*

SCENE FIVE

Dixon-Brown's office at the CAPE Institute. Big windows look out over bushland. The institute is attached to a small provincial university.

Lights come up to reveal DIXON-BROWN *on the floor in a yoga pose.*

She is wearing earbuds—listening to a meditation tape.

The desk blocks her view of the door.

There is a knock.

More knocking.

The door opens gingerly. HARRY *pokes his head around the door.*

HARRY: Hello?

DIXON-BROWN: Is that you, Alan?

HARRY: [*looking around, confused*] Hello?

> DIXON-BROWN *stands up from behind her desk, looking slightly discombobulated.*

DIXON-BROWN: Sorry. Meditating. I've decided this is the only way to deal with my IT traumas. I'm not going to get stressed. I'm just going to breathe.

When I came in this morning, this [*computer*] said, 'Windows Memory Diagnostic Disabled'. It's not even a sentence.

HARRY: I'm Harry.

DIXON-BROWN: Pardon?

HARRY: Harry Jewell.
DIXON-BROWN: Did Alan send you?
HARRY: I'm Harry.
DIXON-BROWN: From IT?
HARRY: From Powerhouse.
DIXON-BROWN: Are you my ten o'clock? Come in. Sorry. My PA has just deserted me. She's decided to have her baby six weeks early.
HARRY: How insensitive.
DIXON-BROWN: Zero commitment to the workplace.
HARRY: Young people.
DIXON-BROWN: Who needs them?

    HARRY *laughs.*

HARRY: If my computer said, 'Windows Memory Diagnostic Disabled', I could become quite … irrational.
DIXON-BROWN: You call IT and they tell you to turn your computer off. And then turn it on again. They go to university for three years, these people, so they can tell you that.
HARRY: I just lie. I tell them I've already tried that.
DIXON-BROWN: Ah. But they know. They can tell from their end. Heather Dixon-Brown. How can I help?
HARRY: I've come to talk to you about a project I have in mind.
DIXON-BROWN: Please.

    She indicates he take a seat.

What sort of project?
HARRY: I want to launch a program to save the tiger quoll.

    The phone rings. DIXON-BROWN *puts on her glasses and looks at the display window to see who's ringing.*

DIXON-BROWN: Sorry, it's Alan Dodd. The turn-on, turn-off man. Do you mind? I'll be one second.

    HARRY *gestures with his upturned palm: 'Go right ahead'.*

[*On the phone*] Alan …
    No need to apologise.
    …
    No, I'd like to be here.
    …

Yes. Say ten-fifteen.

...

Thanks, Alan.

She hangs up.

Alan.

Which means that you're Piper's quoll man. Of course!

HARRY *smiles.*

HARRY: That's me.

DIXON-BROWN: We have your dead quoll here in the lab. It's created quite a lot of excitement.

HARRY: As long as it's not the last one.

DIXON-BROWN: I'm sure there are one or two more out there.

Beat.

So you want to save the tiger quoll? You do realise they haven't been seen in the Otways for a decade. Not even as roadkill. Until you came along.

That's a pretty sure sign that the numbers are too low to be sustainable.

HARRY: According to the Dixon-Brown Index.

DIXON-BROWN: You've done your reading.

HARRY: I liked the sound of your index. Showed me you were living in the real world.

DIXON-BROWN: No point squandering your money on a creature that has passed the point of no return. I'm an ecologist. Not an environmentalist. Use my head, not my heart.

HARRY: Sounds good to me.

DIXON-BROWN: We have to be careful not to dramatise ourselves as saviours; snatching a poor little animal from the jaws of extinction. It makes us feel good. But we rarely succeed.

HARRY: But *sometimes* we do.

DIXON-BROWN: As I say, rarely. Species are like commodities, Mr Jewell. You should only invest in those that are going to give you a good return. In any case, I just don't approve of this 'charismatic fauna' push—making celebrities out of pandas and polar bears.

HARRY: What have you got against pandas?

DIXON-BROWN: They're far too cute. They take people's minds off the real challenge. We need to understand whole ecosystems.

HARRY: That's why I'm proposing a cat eradication program.

DIXON-BROWN: Good luck.

HARRY: A comprehensive survey of all the plants and animals. You could do that.

DIXON-BROWN: It's why we're here.

HARRY: Followed by habitat restoration. I want to see that forest restored to its former glory.

DIXON-BROWN: All very ambitious.

HARRY: I don't have a problem with ambition. Do you?

DIXON-BROWN: And how do you imagine I would fund this crusade, Mr Jewell?

HARRY: Through my company. Powerhouse.

DIXON-BROWN *appears not to know what he's referring to.*

Mining.

DIXON-BROWN: Oh. And what do you mine?

HARRY: Coal. Mostly.

DIXON-BROWN: Ah.

An institute committed to ecology accepting money from the biggest greenhouse polluters on the planet. Some people might think that was compromising, Mr Jewell.

HARRY: And what do you think?

DIXON-BROWN: I think it's dirty money.

HARRY: I know what you're up against. It's been my experience that most academics are glass-half-empty people.

DIXON-BROWN: Tell me about it.

HARRY: We need scientists to stop being gloom-and-doom merchants.

DIXON-BROWN: We need scientists to do the science.

HARRY: I thought universities were strapped for cash.

DIXON-BROWN: We are. But we're not guns for hire. My scientists are fully engaged with their own research. They can't just stop their important work to take up pet projects.

HARRY: Have you ever met a tiger quoll?

DIXON-BROWN: Not a live one.

HARRY: They're not cuddly. They're ferocious.

DIXON-BROWN: So what's the attraction?
HARRY: I grew up with them.
> We sort of had one as a pet. Most nights after dinner we'd see him running along the roof of the milking shed and down the drainpipe.
> One night we were sitting at the dinner table. He climbs through the window, onto my sister's shoulder, then down her arm onto the table. Helps himself to a chicken wing off her plate.

DIXON-BROWN: Cute.
HARRY: Two million dollars. Just to get you started. It's on the table.
DIXON-BROWN: This is not a casino.
HARRY: But we're both willing to take a risk. I can tell that about you.
DIXON-BROWN: Why do you care so much, Mr Jewell?
HARRY: Harry.
DIXON-BROWN: Why do you care so much, Harry?
HARRY: Did you grow up here?
DIXON-BROWN: No.
HARRY: Mum's people were sheep farmers and Dad's were timber cutters. I come from people who've always earned a living off the land. The greenies hate people like us. But my grandfather understood this forest. He respected it. He allowed the mystery of it to be part of his life.
DIXON-BROWN: So you *are* being sentimental.
HARRY: Perhaps.

He smiles.

Long pause.

I was happy when the tiger quolls were running about.
But I mean what I say. The world has changed. And mining has to change with it.

Longer pause.

DIXON-BROWN: How long are you in town?

A knock on the door.

That'll be Alan.
If we're very quiet, he might go away.
HARRY: What about your 'Windows Memory Diagnostic Disabled'?

Beat.

DIXON-BROWN: Would you like to have dinner with me tonight?
HARRY: I'm on a six o'clock flight.
DIXON-BROWN: Cancel it.

SCENE SIX

The animal shelter.

It is late afternoon.

ANDY *enters. He is wearing boxer shorts. His hair is tousled.*

ANDY: Just stay!

>PIPER *appears looking definitely post-coital. She is wearing one of his t-shirts ('Vets Do It Better').*

PIPER: I can't.

>*She picks up her possum and cradles it.*

[*To the possum*] Hello, lovely.
ANDY: Why not?
PIPER: Your sister has arranged it. Some meeting.
ANDY: Take the car, then. I don't like you riding on the Great Ocean Road at night.
PIPER: [*pleased*] Andy, I've ridden a hundred thousand miles on that motorbike.
ANDY: Just take the car.
PIPER: Okay.

>*He puts his arms around her. They kiss.*

ANDY: You are so ... *gifted.*
PIPER: Yeah, right.
ANDY: You *are*. That was unbelievably nice.
PIPER: High praise. Coming from you.
ANDY: That was right up there.
PIPER: Top hundred?
ANDY: Top ten. Easy.
PIPER: Who were the other nine?
ANDY: All with you.

PIPER: No, they weren't.
ANDY: Well, there was that very cute little nurse. What was her name? Can't remember, but gorgeous. With a really beautiful—
PIPER: Once seven is seven, two sevens are fourteen, three sevens are twenty-one, four sevens are—
ANDY: Twenty-nine.
PIPER: —twenty-nine. Twenty-eight! Brute.

ANDY ('the Brute') embraces her and kisses her.

ANDY: Ring my sister and say you have a very urgent series of follow-up meetings which will go on most of the night.
PIPER: She already thinks there's something weird about us.
ANDY: Weird is good.
PIPER: Andy. What if I didn't go back to San Diego at the end of the year?
ANDY: I thought you were keen to try out your love potion on your American koalas.
PIPER: Sure. But what if—you know—I came back?
ANDY: You just want me for sex.
PIPER: Sure. I want you for sex. But—
ANDY: Pipe, we've always said, 'Two years'.
PIPER: What happens if one of us wants to extend?
ANDY: Your life is set on the most amazing course. Don't get stuck here.
PIPER: I love it here.

Beat.

ANDY: Sure. Okay.
PIPER: Maybe you don't *see* it anymore.

She looks out the window.

The kangaroos and wallabies that come boinging in, in the late afternoon. The rainforest. And the ocean just down the road. The old scribbly gum trees. Adorable little koalas. The freshest air anyone could ever breathe. And the people—so funny and kind. And real. This is paradise, Andy.
ANDY: [*teasing about the possum*] This is kidnapping.
PIPER: Don't change the topic.
ANDY: Its mother is probably beside herself.
PIPER: There's no sign of a mother. Anywhere.

ANDY: How many times did you get up last night to feed it?
PIPER: Five.
ANDY: You're a madwoman.
PIPER: We're good for each other. I'm sick of one day at a time. I love you.
ANDY: Piper.
PIPER: I'm serious.
ANDY: I'm not good for you.
PIPER: Why not?
ANDY: There's something wrong with me.
PIPER: Just say it. Say, 'I love you. I want to marry you and have babies and live in a house together.'
ANDY: I can't give you what you want.
PIPER: How do you know?
ANDY: I can't commit for the long haul, Pipe. I can't explain why. I'm not that sort of person.
PIPER: I'm not the woman you want to do it with. That's the truth, isn't it?

Beat.

ANDY: Some creatures survive perfectly well on their own.
   A possum has all the instincts it needs to survive, you know.
PIPER: Like you. Mister Solitary.
ANDY: Yes.
PIPER: So I should understand that this relationship has no future.

He moves to embrace her.

Don't.

SCENE SEVEN

Dixon-Brown's apartment.

HARRY *and* DIXON-BROWN *are seated at the table, drinking gin and tonics and enjoying each other's company.*

HARRY: So. Divorced?
DIXON-BROWN: Not quite. I have the papers in there.
HARRY: Can't bring yourself to sign them?
DIXON-BROWN: Silly, isn't it? You know something? I went swimming on that stinking hot day last week. At Urquhart's Bluff. And when I

came out of the surf, I looked down and my wedding ring was gone. After twenty-two years.

HARRY: The fates have spoken. Do the paperwork.

DIXON-BROWN: I shall. Absolutely. This weekend.

HARRY: Any kids?

DIXON-BROWN: One son. Max. He's a skiing instructor in the Italian alps.

HARRY: Gee, that's tough.

DIXON-BROWN: He used to live with us here. It seemed like every morning he'd stride bare-chested into the kitchen with a different half-clad girl.

Then one morning I was making the coffee and he barrels in with two girls.

HARRY: Wow.

DIXON-BROWN: That was my husband's reaction. Green with envy. I said to my son, 'Max, maybe it's time you found a place on your own'. But he didn't take any notice. It was my husband who decided to move out.

HARRY: When was that?

DIXON-BROWN: Three years ago.

HARRY: That sounds like your party story. What really happened?

DIXON-BROWN: I stopped wanting him.

HARRY: I don't know how people keep it going.

DIXON-BROWN: Neither do I. Would you believe I wrote X-E-S on my side of the bed? It was to remind myself to have sex with him.

There is a buzz from the intercom. DIXON-BROWN *crosses to it.*

PIPER: [*on the intercom*] Hi, Dix.

DIXON-BROWN: Piper. Come on up.

[To HARRY] Does this happen to you often? Complete strangers tell you their most intimate secrets.

HARRY: [*smiling charmingly*] You're not a complete stranger.

DIXON-BROWN: Tell me about your wife? Stephanie. Does she work?

HARRY: She used to be a primary school teacher. But that was a long time ago. She doesn't need to work. She's Clovis Carter's niece.

DIXON-BROWN: Sheesh. Is that how you got into mining? You married a Carter?

HARRY: No. I built Powerhouse from scratch. But Uncle Clovis did manage to muscle his way onto my board.

DIXON-BROWN: Is he as big a bastard as they say?
HARRY: Nah. He's a pussycat. You just have to tickle his tummy.

DIXON-BROWN shudders.

A knock at the door.

Should I steel myself?
DIXON-BROWN: You invited her. Probably.

She opens the door. PIPER enters. She is wearing a black cocktail dress. She is transformed.

PIPER: Hi.
DIXON-BROWN: You look … amazing.
HARRY: Piper.
PIPER: Mr Evil.

HARRY laughs.

DIXON-BROWN: You didn't bring Andy?
PIPER: No.

DIXON-BROWN gives her a look.

I'll tell you later.
HARRY: Is this the vet?
PIPER: Yes.
DIXON-BROWN: My brother.
HARRY: Oh! Shit! Andy is your brother?
DIXON-BROWN: He is.
HARRY: Great guy. Amazing. Tough. Stubborn.
DIXON-BROWN: Rude.
HARRY: Rude. [*To* PIPER] He's your partner?
PIPER: No. We're just ships in the night.
DIXON-BROWN: Oh, gawd.
They've been together for two years.
HARRY: Oh.
DIXON-BROWN: They met in Africa.
PIPER: Zambia.
HARRY: Doing what?
PIPER: Tracking wild dogs. Well, that's what I was doing. Andy was working with the Zambian Wildlife Authority.

DIXON-BROWN: Treating elephants. [*Pointedly to* HARRY] Those African wild dogs are endangered. They're on the Red List.
PIPER: But their population has made a big comeback, Dix. Case in point. That was a population way below five thousand. Virtually no sightings. But gradually, gradually they're coming back up.
HARRY: Okay. So you've had experience working with endangered animals?

HARRY *and* DIXON-BROWN *exchange meaningful glances.*

I didn't realise this was such a family affair. Champagne?
PIPER: Are we celebrating?
HARRY: We certainly are.

He pours champagne into her glass.

We're celebrating our friendship.
DIXON-BROWN: Cheers. To us.

They clink glasses.

PIPER: You're more chirpy than the last time I saw you. You both are.
HARRY: I had dinner with my daughter last night. You were right about the emotional roller-coaster of fourteen-year-old girls. I am now forgiven and my daughter has decided that I am the superior parent.
PIPER: And so begins a lifetime of competition between you and your wife.
HARRY: No. My daughter's just so excited about the tiger quoll project. She wants to come down and volunteer—
PIPER: What tiger quoll project?

Beat.

DIXON-BROWN: CAPE is going to oversee a project to save the quolls.
PIPER: Powerhouse Mining involved in this?
DIXON-BROWN: It's the biggest biodiversity monitoring program we've ever undertaken.
HARRY: We'll claw this species back from the brink.
PIPER: If there are any out there.
HARRY: 'If there's one, there'll be more.'
DIXON-BROWN: The issue—as I understand it, Pipe—is that they're hard to find. They're shy. Plus they're nocturnal and they can move quickly over vast distances in the forest.

I'm thinking we could base this on a scat analysis. Like you did with the dogs in Africa.

HARRY: Which means?

PIPER: Quolls use communal latrine sites.

HARRY: They all shit in the one place? Fascinating. So how would we find their poo?

PIPER: You'd train dogs.

HARRY: Like the ones at the airport?

PIPER: Except you'd have to train them to detect tiger quoll poo.

HARRY: But how do you get the poo—to train them?

PIPER: Ah. Good point. There are tiger quolls in captivity. In zoos.

HARRY: Right. So we buy a truckload of poo from the zoo.

PIPER: No, you bring in some live quolls. Keep them in an enclosure—and collect their scats. Nice and fresh. Then you train your dogs to sniff out the poo.

HARRY: It's very *basic* all this, isn't it?

PIPER: Mm hm. Then you take the dogs into the forest. Find the latrine sites. And you've found your quolls.

HARRY: But we need to know how many quolls.

PIPER: Oh, yes you do. So you do a DNA analysis of the scats. Because each animal has a unique DNA obviously—you can determine how many animals are using each latrine site. There might be twenty or thirty.

HARRY: And you'd compile a population census from there. Sweet.

PIPER: But of course you'd need to find five thousand quolls to make it worth your while. Wouldn't you, Dix?

DIXON-BROWN: Move on.

HARRY: I think what she's trying to say is don't look a gift horse in the mouth.

PIPER: Listen. There has not been a confirmed sighting of one of these animals in the Otways for ten years.

HARRY: Until I blundered along.

PIPER: One dead tiger quoll.

HARRY: And a massive project to find the remaining population.

PIPER: And to mine coal.

HARRY: We're not mining the forest.

PIPER: Okay. Destroying agricultural land, then.

HARRY: I give you my word, I'll do everything in my power to restore this forest to how it was when the quolls were running about.
　　And something else. The coal industry. Its days are numbered. Take the money now, while it's being offered.
DIXON-BROWN: We want you to run the project.
PIPER: No way!

     END OF ACT ONE

ACT TWO

SCENE ONE

Night. The Australian rainforest.

A tent is illuminated—a small intimate space in the vast blackness.

The sounds of a hot summer night: crickets and a couple of distant owls.

Inside the tent, two naked people are making love in silhouette. The sexual energy progresses from tender to frenzied; it peaks and then stills.

PIPER *emerges from the tent, and pokes the fire.*

PIPER: You do believe in global warming, don't you?

The man half emerges. It is HARRY. *He is bare-chested.*

HARRY: That is one thing you really should have checked.

He climbs out of the tent.

I think it's thirty-four per cent of greenhouse gas comes from burning coal.

Maybe thirty-seven per cent. I'll bring my notes next time.

PIPER: How do you know there's gonna be a next time?

HARRY: Because when you make love like that, you wanna do it again.

PIPER: Let me get this straight.

HARRY: I make a shitload of money.

PIPER: Is that supposed to be erotic?

HARRY: It's pretty erotic.

PIPER *breaks away.*

PIPER: This isn't going to work, Harry.

HARRY: Hey. Come on.

PIPER: I've made a mistake.

I'm not a very good judge.

The day after my dad died, I met this guy in a bar in Brooklyn. We had sex twice and then a week later he was on the news—holding up a convenience store.

HARRY: I'm pretty straight up and down, Piper.

PIPER: You're the most confusing person I ever met.
HARRY: [*pleased*] Really?

She punches him.

The gentle whoosh of an owl. They watch it as it flies over their heads.

PIPER: Oh, look. See?
HARRY: Whoa!

They watch.

PIPER: An owl!
HARRY: A barking owl. He's a beauty.
PIPER: It's a big one. You sure it's not a powerful owl?
HARRY: Maybe. Hard to tell 'em apart.
PIPER: I think the barking owl has vertical stripes in the front. This one's more horizontal. See.
HARRY: Yep. You're El Supremo. The archduke of the predators.
PIPER: This is a lucky sign. If he's in the forest, there must be enough prey to sustain him.
HARRY: He can eat a possum, that fella.
PIPER: He'll have a nest in a hollow tree close by.
HARRY: Good news for the quolls. Plenty to eat. Somewhere to live.
PIPER: I hope so.
  I love the birds here.

The owl flies off.

  Oh, there he goes.
HARRY: I'm not used to this either, you know. I've been married for fifteen years, remember.
PIPER: I know. I'm sorry. You end up with a loon on your first date.
HARRY: I end up with a mysterious, intriguing woman.

Beat.

PIPER: Oh, man. I knew this was a dumb thing to do.
HARRY: Piper, I think you need to give it a chance.
PIPER: That's ridiculous. You're my boss.
HARRY: Heather Dixon-Brown is your boss.
PIPER: I don't want her knowing about this.

Hannah Day as Piper and Matt Dyktynski as Harry in Black Swan State Theatre Company's 2015 production of EXTINCTION. (Photo: Gary Marsh)

HARRY: I'm not tellin' her.

   PIPER *is relieved.*

Look. You know what money means? It means a big life.
PIPER: I thought you wanted a simple life.
HARRY: That's why I love mining. It's big and it's simple.
   You find minerals—dig 'em up—and sell them. By the shipload.
   So many people, they lead such myopic lives. They agonise about building a fence, paving a driveway. But I've built highways and bridges and railroads.
PIPER: Exactly. You're the problem.
HARRY: If you want to make a difference to 'the environment', you have to be rich.
   This mine comes wrapped in a fifty-year plan. Return here when you're an old lady, Piper. You won't see a trace of the mine. The cats'll be gone. And the quolls will be back, ruling the forest.
PIPER: This is not about one Master of the Universe saving the planet. This is about everyone transforming the way they live.
HARRY: Yeah, sure. Change the light bulbs. Save your lunch wrap. Take your own scruffy bag to the supermarket.
PIPER: That's making a difference.
HARRY: Piper. Most people don't have time to be the idealists you want them to be. They're too busy paying off the mortgage and feeding their kids.
PIPER: Maybe you hang with the wrong crowd. I know heaps of people who spend their weekends planting trees or cleaning up riverbanks.

They hear the screech of a white cockatoo flying above.

HARRY: I love this place. I've been away far too long.

   Long pause.

PIPER: Was your wife turned on by the cash?
HARRY: Not so turned on by me, apparently.
PIPER: Your friend Damien Gore—is he wealthy?
HARRY: He's a friggin' poet.
PIPER: See, women don't care about the money.
HARRY: What planet do you live on?
PIPER: They don't.

We live in such different worlds. That's why this relationship can't work.

HARRY: It's not a relationship. It's just sex.

PIPER: Oh well, that's clear, then.

HARRY: Piper!

PIPER: That's fine. That's good.

HARRY: Piper? I do want this to be more than just sex.

PIPER: It's only a month since you split up with your wife. You don't think it's a bit soon.

HARRY: There's no waiting period. It's not dental insurance.

PIPER: I just don't want you to have unreal expectations—that's all.

As soon as this project's done, I'm outta here.

HARRY: Is that the arrangement you had with the vet?

PIPER: Yep.

HARRY: And that's finished?

PIPER: Oh, yeah. He's made that very clear.

HARRY: [*hearing her wounded tone*] Ahhh.

PIPER: Let's set up the cameras. That's what we're here for.

HARRY: Andy's a good bloke. Hardworking, knows his stuff. He was probably right about putting down that quoll. I shouldn't have bawled him out.

But I know the type—knew him the moment he came through that door.

He's the kind of greenie who's always saying no. No dams. No mines. No roads.

You've got to believe in your own species, Piper. In the human capacity to achieve great things.

PIPER: This is a bit rich, don't you think?

Coming from you.

HARRY: Look, I am not some multinational corporation devouring the Amazon. I'm just a bloke who's come back home. I know what I'm doing here. What I don't understand is what you're doing here.

PIPER: In Australia?

HARRY: In this forest. Saving other people's animals? It's like you're burdening yourself with the responsibility of keeping everything alive—

PIPER: You think there's something wrong with me because I care about sick animals?

HARRY: It's the dying that worries you, isn't it?
PIPER: Maybe we should have breakfast.
HARRY: You're frightened of it.
PIPER: Everybody's frightened of it.
HARRY: I never think about it.
PIPER: Yeah well, you're a special case. You're invincible.
HARRY: How come you're so defensive?
PIPER: I am not!

Beat.

You make me defensive.
HARRY: I'm sorry. I won't mention it, again.

He holds up a frying pan.

Breakfast?

He busies himself.

Nothing like eggs and bacon fried on a camp fire.
PIPER: I don't do bacon.
HARRY: Of course you don't!

He reaches into his pack and produces a packet of bacon.

Just as well I brought some.
PIPER: When I'm with you, I become like this humourless ideologue. Which I'm not with other people.
HARRY: Why do you think that is?
PIPER: People are not independent entities. We all exist in relationship with one another. You're a businessman polluting the planet.
HARRY: Why don't you just think about me as a great fuck? Then *in relationship*, you're a great fuck and we're all happy.
PIPER: [*affectionately*] You're a great fucker. That's what you are.
Let's put this [*camera*] up there. Can you reach that branch?
HARRY: I thought we were having breakfast.
PIPER: These cameras are triggered by movement. I put in ten at Stumpy Gully: I got one thousand photographs of Mitchell grass blowing in the wind.
HARRY: Oh, no.

PIPER switches on the monitor which shows what the camera is looking at—the forest late at night.

PIPER: I think we should try some of these cameras pointing back into the trees. Since the quolls are such good climbers.
HARRY: Good idea. How many of these gadgets have we got?
PIPER: Sixty.
HARRY: [*placing the camera*] Here?
PIPER: [*watching the monitor*] That way a bit. Left. Bit more. Bit more. Ah, too far. That's it. That's good.

> HARRY *attaches the camera to a branch.*

HARRY: What have you decided about Beast?
PIPER: He's booked in to have the operation next week.
HARRY: Whoa. Great.
PIPER: Andy is very disapproving, of course.
HARRY: It's not his dog.
PIPER: That's right.

> *Beat.*

Do you think I'm doing the wrong thing? Just delaying facing the inevitable?
HARRY: [*with a shrug*] I think you've got a lot of grief in that big heart of yours.
PIPER: My mother had this friend Betty, right? They were like best friends. For twenty-five years. Then Betty's son, Axel, jumped off the roof of his Upper East Side apartment. My mother goes, 'I can't deal with suicide'. Like Betty was way more equipped and didn't need her best friend to call or hold her hand. My mother just went AWOL.
  I don't want to be that person.
HARRY: But you're not. You looked after your dad. For two years.
PIPER: I want to be a person who faces up to things. If you can't face death, you can't face life. Right?
HARRY: Caring for your dog, so that he can enjoy a few more years of life. That's not wrong. Or weak. That's a testament of love.
PIPER: I'm sorry, Harry. I just don't know what I'm doing here, anymore.
  I really did think Andy and I had something going?
HARRY: Why don't you go and see Beast?
PIPER: You mean, go home?

HARRY *pokes the fire.*

HARRY: Just check in for a week or so?
PIPER: Really?
HARRY: Why not?
PIPER: Just jump on a plane?
HARRY: Mm hm.
PIPER: What about my carbon footprint?
HARRY: We'll plant some trees.
PIPER: [*clearly excited*] I could just book a ticket?
HARRY: Yep. Do it. Book two. I'll come with you.
PIPER: Harry.
HARRY: Why not?
PIPER: You don't even know me.
HARRY: I wouldn't mind a few days in New York.
PIPER: You can't get everything you want, you know.
HARRY: Why not?
PIPER: Life isn't like that.
HARRY: Mine is.

Come on. Let's rustle up some breakfast.

SCENE TWO

The animal shelter.

ANDY *enters. He is wearing a white coat and carrying a travelling box containing a cat. He puts it on the table and peers in through a small hole.*

ANDY: How's it going, Schrödinger?

Beat.

That'll teach you to get involved with a snake.

He peruses the medicine shelf.

Tempazadine. Here we go. One tablet a day. Don't drive and don't use heavy machinery.

He peers into the box again.

Hey, look sharp. Your old man's out there and he's very keen to see you.

There is a knock at the door and DIXON-BROWN *appears.*

What are you doing here?

DIXON-BROWN: Thanks for that warm greeting. I've just driven three hours down the Great Ocean Road.

ANDY: I'm working.

DIXON-BROWN: You've broken up with Piper.

ANDY: News travels fast.

DIXON-BROWN: Mum told me.

ANDY: I draw the line at claiming coalmining is good for the environment.

DIXON-BROWN: Who's making that claim?

ANDY *shakes his head and picks up the cat in the box.*

Is that a cat?

ANDY: [*to the cat*] Are you a cat?

DIXON-BROWN: There is a cat in there, Andy.

ANDY: I am a vet, Heather.

DIXON-BROWN: You—the great advocate for our native flora and fauna—are patching up cats.

ANDY: It's a pet. He was suffering. I cured him.

He walks offstage to the reception area.

[*Off*] Hey, prof. Here he is. Old Schrödinger. One hundred per cent alive. Make sure you keep him in at night, okay?

ANDY *returns.*

DIXON-BROWN: I brought you some food.

ANDY: She was just my girlfriend, Dix. She didn't like *cook* or anything. I am perfectly capable of looking after myself.

DIXON-BROWN: Mum sent you some strawberry jam.

ANDY: Very kind.

DIXON-BROWN: Tomato pickles. Peaches. Pâté. Cheese. That Persian fetta you like.

ANDY: There's a supermarket two miles down the road. I don't need food parcels.

DIXON-BROWN: Andy?

ANDY: I don't need *a carer.*

Beat.

DIXON-BROWN: We just thought you might need some cheering up.
ANDY: That's a joke. That really is.

Beat.

DIXON-BROWN: So whose decision was it, to break up?
ANDY: Not that it's any of your business.
DIXON-BROWN: Whose decision?
ANDY: I don't want to be with someone who would even contemplate environmental vandalism on the scale you two are planning.

DIXON-BROWN *splutters.*

DIXON-BROWN: We are restoring the forest! The disappearance of the tiger quoll is just the tip of the iceberg.
ANDY: I'll say it is.
DIXON-BROWN: We are monitoring the entire bioregion, Andy. One hundred and sixty thousand hectares. Ninety-two rare and threatened species.
ANDY: If you don't rein in your CO_2 emissions, you won't have a bioregion!

Nor any icebergs.

DIXON-BROWN: Andy!

ANDY *picks up the box of groceries. As he swings around, the box slips from his arms and the produce scatters on the floor. He is shocked.*

Here. Let me.
ANDY: Leave it.
DIXON-BROWN: I'll do it.
ANDY: Leave it.
DIXON-BROWN: I'll get a broom.
ANDY: [*shouting*] Leave it! Leave me alone. I don't want you here.
DIXON-BROWN: Don't treat me like this, Andy.
ANDY: 'Don't treat me like this, Andy.'
DIXON-BROWN: Oh, for godsake. Hundreds of institutions are funded by mining money.
ANDY: So? Are you stupid as well as corrupt?
DIXON-BROWN: Don't push it. Just don't. Okay? Don't. Because if I turn my back—

ANDY: So, how big's the cheque, professor?

During the next sequence, he repacks the box with the grocery items scattered across the floor.

DIXON-BROWN: Mind your own business. Here, let me do that, for godsake.

He lets her take over.

ANDY: See? You can't even be transparent with your own family.

DIXON-BROWN: Two point eight million dollars.

ANDY *gestures: 'I rest my case'.*

DIXON-BROWN *mimics the gesture.*

It's not a secret. It's on their website.

ANDY *repeats the gesture.*

Money has to come from somewhere—

ANDY: Not from coalmining, professor.

DIXON-BROWN: —as most grown-up people understand.

You want me to close the CAPE. Is that what you want? Then we can all bask in ideological purity. Andy, this is a massive project. One that will deliver major outcomes to the forest.

ANDY: There is no point delivering *major outcomes to the forest* if Harry Jewell keeps spewing crap into the atmosphere.

DIXON-BROWN: Every person on this planet wants to find a solution to the energy crisis, Andy. Not just you. Even the energy sector wants a solution.

ANDY: No, they don't.

DIXON-BROWN: Of course they do. You think you're the only musketeer in the story.

ANDY: Big Coal does not give a stuff about climate change.

DIXON-BROWN: And yet people have to be able to turn the lights on, across the globe. Not just here. Even you would have to acknowledge that.

ANDY: Oh my God, you really have bought into their propaganda.

Once again he drops an item.

Shit.

He clutches the side of the desk.

DIXON-BROWN: I don't know why we're having this fight. Your splitting with Piper has nothing to do with fossil fuels. I came down to see if I could help you patch things up.

ANDY: I don't want to patch things up.

Pause.

DIXON-BROWN: It's going to be very lonely up there on the moral high ground.

An automatic bell indicates that someone has come into the waiting room.

ANDY: Excuse me. I have a client.

ANDY *moves towards the door.* DIXON-BROWN *catches his arm.*

DIXON-BROWN: Listen, Andy, I'm gonna be blunt—

ANDY: No, I'm gonna be blunt—

ANDY *closes the door to the waiting room firmly so they cannot be heard.*

DIXON-BROWN: You need me. Don't do this. Don't drive me away.

He takes her arm and pulls her across the surgery so they can have this out in private.

ANDY: [*hissing*] I have a disease.

DIXON-BROWN: Andy, you're making a mistake.

ANDY: Did you hear me? I have a terminal illness.

DIXON-BROWN: I know that.

ANDY: A genetic disease—

DIXON-BROWN: I know.

ANDY: Which you don't have.

DIXON-BROWN: Look, Andy, I understand what you're going through—

ANDY: No, you don't. You have no idea. It's not happening to you.

DIXON-BROWN: But I live with it— Stop it, Andy. You're hurting my arm.

ANDY: I'm the one who inherited the mutation. Not you.

DIXON-BROWN: Yes, alright. It's not happening to me.

ANDY: No, it's not. It's happening in *my* body.

DIXON-BROWN: Yes, Andy.

ANDY: In every cell. Of my body.

DIXON-BROWN: Stop this! Hey. Stop it! Don't push me. Ow! Listen, you shithead, I'm the one who's gonna have to fucking look after you.

ANDY: Oh! Excuse me?
DIXON-BROWN: I'm sorry. I didn't mean—
ANDY: Oh, yes you did.
DIXON-BROWN: No, Andy, I didn't—
ANDY: What a burden for you.
DIXON-BROWN: That's not what I meant.
ANDY: What a rod for your back.
DIXON-BROWN: I'm sorry, Andy.
ANDY: Being sorry is totally fucking useless. I am not going to be your 'onerous responsibility'. I'm not playin' that game. Is that understood?
DIXON-BROWN: Andy!
ANDY: You are relieved of any obligations toward me from this day onwards. Let's make that very clear.
DIXON-BROWN: You need me—
ANDY: I do not. And another thing.

    I don't have time to pander to social niceties. I don't have time to debate the pros and cons of university funding arrangements. You're destroying the forest and the earth and I will fight you until the day I can no longer stand up or form words that make sense.

    I won't have a relationship with anyone who is prepared to be a pin-up girl for coalmining. And even though you're my sister, you have to know, you did this. You destroyed the relationship between us.

He ushers her out the door and slams it firmly.

Lights off on ANDY.

DIXON-BROWN *bumps into* PIPER *who is just coming in. They both jump in shock.*

PIPER: Dix!   DIXON-BROWN: Piper!
PIPER & DIXON-BROWN: [*together*] What are you doing here?
PIPER: I left my iron.
DIXON-BROWN: Oh.
PIPER: And my breadmaker.
DIXON-BROWN: Right.
PIPER: And some clothes.

    Beat.

Are you alright?

DIXON-BROWN: [*she's not*] Yeah.
PIPER: Andy's not here?
DIXON-BROWN: He's in there.
PIPER: It's Wednesday. He usually goes into town on Wednesdays.

    DIXON-BROWN *shrugs*.

DIXON-BROWN: I wouldn't go in if I were you. He's pretty agitated.
PIPER: What about?
DIXON-BROWN: Coalmining.
PIPER: He never lets up.
DIXON-BROWN: He's up against it, Piper. I can't—
PIPER: Andy's okay when he's *protesting*. He's the kind of person who's always saying no. No dams. No mines. No roads. But you have to step up to make things happen. You've got to believe in your own species.
DIXON-BROWN: Really?
PIPER: Oh. Just for your information, I told … er … Harry Jewell that I'm fully committed to the Powerhouse project.
DIXON-BROWN: When did you do that?
PIPER: Yesterday. I, he came with me … we got the new cameras yesterday.
DIXON-BROWN: Sorry. I'm not following.
PIPER: The delivery arrived. Of the cameras we ordered? So we decided to get started. We went down to Stony Creek and installed them. The new software is brilliant. I can access the cameras on my own phone. The phone just goes bing whenever a camera detects movement. Bing! Up pops an image. Hopefully of a tiger quoll. See?

    PIPER *shows* DIXON-BROWN *her phone. An image of the forest appears on the back wall.*

DIXON-BROWN: Is that the only problem between you and Andy?
PIPER: What?
DIXON-BROWN: Harry Jewell.

    Beat.

PIPER: What do you mean?
DIXON-BROWN: I'm feeling uneasy—
PIPER: About what?
DIXON-BROWN: Listen, Piper, I feel responsible for talking you into this tiger quoll business—
PIPER: You didn't talk me into it.

DIXON-BROWN: You know I did. And it's just a wild goose chase.
PIPER: According to the Dixon-Brown Index.
DIXON-BROWN: According to any sensible person's assessment. We're not just talking about any apex predator with low densities. This is a population which could be non-existent here. It's madness throwing your best people at something like this.

Whereas addressing the causes of the decline of the manna gum woodlands. That's real. That has to be prioritised because there are demonstrable outcomes. Restore the habitat. Ensure the future of the koalas on the Cape.
PIPER: There is no more funding. You've made that abundantly clear.
DIXON-BROWN: For godsake, Piper. There will be money. I will find money.
PIPER: I'm not dropping the tiger quoll project.
DIXON-BROWN: This is not about your career. It's about your life.
PIPER: My life?

Oh, I see.

My life is fine. Andy is fine. The weather is fine. Yep. We're all just fine. Except that Andy does not want to have a relationship with me. He may not have mentioned this to you, Dix. But he has made that abundantly clear to me.

I have tried everything I can to make this work. I don't know what more I can do.
DIXON-BROWN: There is something you need to know about Andy.
PIPER: [*snapping*] What?

ANDY *opens the door with a box which he shoves into* PIPER*'s arms.*

ANDY: Here's your stuff. Off you go. Both of you. I have clients in here with sick animals.
PIPER: [*shouting*] What is the matter with you?! You are such an emotional retard!

ANDY *slams the door closed.*

Beat.

DIXON-BROWN: What time did you get back to town, last night? You and Harry?
PIPER: We didn't get back until the morning. We camped.

DIXON-BROWN: You camped out?
PIPER: In separate tents. Of course.
DIXON-BROWN: Piper. You've done great work setting this up. We'll find a couple of postgrads to take this on.
PIPER: Postgrads can't do this.
DIXON-BROWN: They can start next year.
PIPER: Next year? What are you talking about? This is not some lifestyle choice; some way of shoring up a salary for myself.
DIXON-BROWN: Nevertheless there are processes.
PIPER: Processes. Jesus Christ. This is our chance to get an important project up and running. And you're pulling the plug.
DIXON-BROWN: I'll clear it all with Harry tonight.
PIPER: Clear what? He doesn't want postgraduates running this.
DIXON-BROWN: I'm the director of the institute. I call the shots.
PIPER: The money is on the table.
DIXON-BROWN: I'm fully aware of that, Piper.
PIPER: He's going back to the Hunter this afternoon.
DIXON-BROWN: He's at a function with me and the vice-chancellor.
PIPER: The planet is emptying. But what do you care? You have to go to drinks with the vice-chancellor. What's it matter if we wake up and half the species on earth are dead? Because your index can't measure how lonely and lost the human race is going to be.

She is about to walk off.

DIXON-BROWN: You're not the only person who cares, okay?
PIPER: Is that so?
DIXON-BROWN: Piper, it would be very, very inappropriate for you to get involved with Harry Jewell. Regardless of the obvious professional compromise, it's never a good idea to get mixed up with a man on the rebound from an ugly separation.
PIPER: I can assure you, there is nothing going on with me and Harry Jewell.

SCENE THREE

Dixon-Brown's apartment. It is late at night.

The intercom buzzer sounds. It rings again. DIXON-BROWN *emerges from her bedroom, pulling on a kimono.*

She crosses to the intercom.

DIXON-BROWN: Andy? What are you doing?
ANDY: [*on the intercom*] Just passing by.
DIXON-BROWN: It's one a.m. What's up?
ANDY: [*on the intercom*] I'm looking at a very clean, very upmarket Range Rover.
DIXON-BROWN: And you felt you needed to share this?
ANDY: [*on the intercom*] Hybrid. Silver colour. Black trim.
DIXON-BROWN: [*to herself*] Shit. [*To* ANDY] Are you alright? I'll come down.
ANDY: [*on the intercom*] No. I know why you're so keen to help me patch things up with Piper. Because that gets you off the hook.
DIXON-BROWN: I'm coming down.
ANDY: [*on the intercom*] No. I wouldn't dream of crashing your party. Gotta dash. Got a cab waiting.
DIXON-BROWN: Andy?

She rushes to the window and sees the cab drive away.

HARRY *appears in his boxer shorts.*

Where did you leave your car?
HARRY: In your parking space.
DIXON-BROWN: Oh, no.
HARRY: You told me to leave it there. Is it okay?
DIXON-BROWN: Does Andy know what kind of car you drive?
HARRY: Was that Andy?
DIXON-BROWN: Does he?
HARRY: No. Why would he?
DIXON-BROWN: That's alright, then.
Want a nightcap?
HARRY: I think I might go back to bed.
DIXON-BROWN: Oh, come on. Just a little one.
HARRY: You sure that's okay? About Andy?

DIXON-BROWN *busies herself pouring drinks.*

DIXON-BROWN: I've had a lot worse boyfriends than you.
HARRY: That's nice to know.

DIXON-BROWN: Piper told me she took delivery of some cameras yesterday.
HARRY: Great.
DIXON-BROWN: I think she went down to install them last night.

Pause.

She's plucky, isn't she? Going into the forest on her own, at night.
HARRY: She won't come to any harm in the forest.
DIXON-BROWN: Still. Pretty vulnerable out there. On her own.
I'd be worried that some psycho might come into my tent.
Did you see your wife last night?
HARRY: No.
DIXON-BROWN: Oh. I thought you were up in the Hunter.
HARRY: I was. Well, I was going to, but Stephanie cancelled on me. She's going through a tough patch. Her relationship isn't going so well.
DIXON-BROWN: Poor Stephanie.
HARRY: She's pretty mad with me.
DIXON-BROWN: Poor you.
HARRY: She'll get over it. Hopefully.
DIXON-BROWN: So, where did you end up last night? Ice?
HARRY: No. Thanks. I went to the hotel.

Beat.

DIXON-BROWN: I'm worried about Piper.
HARRY: Why?
DIXON-BROWN: She's been behaving very oddly. I don't know if you know—she and my brother have split up.
HARRY: That's no good.
DIXON-BROWN: No. It's not good. She really loves him, you know. He's a bit of a hero, my brother.
HARRY: I thought he was the one who pulled the plug?
DIXON-BROWN: I don't think so. He adores her. It's just your coalmine.
By the way, I've got a conference coming up in Queensland. On the Sunshine Coast. I thought you might have some business up there.
HARRY: No.
DIXON-BROWN: Are you sure? I'm staying at the Sheraton. I only have to work for an hour delivering a paper and the rest of the time I'll be lying by the pool sipping cocktails.

HARRY: Sounds lovely. But no.

Beat.

DIXON-BROWN: Why not?

Beat.

HARRY: I think you know.
DIXON-BROWN: No. I don't.
HARRY: You need someone, you deserve someone who wants to be— who's ready for a proper relationship.
DIXON-BROWN: I don't think you should speak for me.
HARRY: Sorry.
DIXON-BROWN: You don't know what I want.
HARRY: Fair enough. I should speak for myself. And I'm not ready for this.
DIXON-BROWN: This?
HARRY: This 'thing' between us. I'm not ready. I'm not comfortable.
DIXON-BROWN: Because … you would prefer a younger person?
HARRY: Don't be silly. You're a very attractive woman.
DIXON-BROWN: But a bit old?
HARRY: No.
DIXON-BROWN: What then?
HARRY: Dix. For heaven's sake, I just told you. I'm not ready for a relationship.
DIXON-BROWN: And who says I am? You're making assumptions here. I'm five years older than you. But that doesn't make me predatory. I don't *need* a relationship.
HARRY: Your age has nothing to do with it. I didn't even know you were older than me.
DIXON-BROWN: Yes, you did. You asked me.
HARRY: I did not.
DIXON-BROWN: You asked me when I was at university. Because you wanted to find out and I told you. I told you the truth.
HARRY: So?
DIXON-BROWN: So?
HARRY: What's it matter?
DIXON-BROWN: It matters to you, obviously.

HARRY: It doesn't. It really doesn't matter.

DIXON-BROWN: What does matter then? Since you are calling this off. I think. Is that what's happening here? You don't want to continue. You don't want to see me anymore.

HARRY: Dix. Come on.

DIXON-BROWN: I just want to know, Harry. I don't play games. If you are rejecting me, I'd like to know why. I think you owe me that. I think you need to say that you would prefer a younger woman—

HARRY: Dix, for godsake.

DIXON-BROWN: Of course!

You've never been with a woman who has pubic hair.

HARRY: Don't be so ridiculous. Of course I have.

DIXON-BROWN: But it's a bit off-putting.

HARRY: I should go.

DIXON-BROWN: Why? Because you can't stomach a woman who stands up to you? That can be a turn-off. I understand that. You're frightened of me. You are. You're shaking in your nylon socks.

HARRY: Oh, Dix. Come here. Come on.

DIXON-BROWN: No. I want to know. Is it Piper? Is that the problem? You're sleeping with Piper as well.

HARRY: No! Of course not.

DIXON-BROWN: Even though you just lied about the hotel.

HARRY: Dix—

DIXON-BROWN: Harry?

HARRY: I went into the forest with Piper last night.

DIXON-BROWN: I know.

HARRY: Did she tell you?

DIXON-BROWN: She told me you slept in separate tents.

Beat.

So why did you come here tonight?

HARRY: I'm sorry.

DIXON-BROWN: You're obviously quite smitten with Piper, then? Is that how she feels?

Beat.

Harry?

HARRY: I don't know.

DIXON-BROWN: Get out of here.

HARRY: Dix. I've been with the same woman for fifteen years. I'm not in the habit of doing this. I was never once unfaithful to my wife.

DIXON-BROWN: What do you want? The Victoria Cross?

HARRY: I thought you wanted the same thing.

DIXON-BROWN: To be humiliated? No. As it happens.

HARRY: That's not what I meant.

DIXON-BROWN: You thought I wanted to compete for your affections. With my brother's girlfriend.

HARRY: No.

DIXON-BROWN: No, you're right. You're a marketplace guy. What's the problem? Everything's about competition. Competition is good. Competition is invigorating.

HARRY: I made a mistake. I'm sorry.

DIXON-BROWN: Sleeping with me?

HARRY: No. Of course not.

DIXON-BROWN: What was the mistake then?

HARRY: Thinking that you were in the market for some … not market. You know what I mean. You were, you were, up for … just having a nice time together.

DIXON-BROWN: But I'm not having a nice time.

HARRY: No. It's taken a bit of a dive.

DIXON-BROWN: Go home. Do whatever you want. To make yourself feel better.

    HARRY *leaves, then turns back.*

HARRY: Life is messy, you know.

DIXON-BROWN: Really.

HARRY: You cannot reduce what happens between people to numbers you record on a chart. I'm sorry to tell you, professor, you can't judge human feeling by algorithms.

DIXON-BROWN: No? And yet here you are: scoring ten out of ten for bastardry.

HARRY: You seem to have reverted to some nineteen-fifties idea of relationships. These days, when you have sex with someone, you are not automatically making a lifelong commitment.

DIXON-BROWN: You did not have sex with some stranger you met on a dating site. You had sex with Piper. I don't care what time zone you live in. That's a betrayal.
HARRY: Piper is a grown-up. It's not like I forced myself on her.
DIXON-BROWN: Yes. Well, there'll be repercussions for Piper.
HARRY: Like what?
DIXON-BROWN: The tragic part, my friend, is that I fell for your scam.
HARRY: What repercussions?
DIXON-BROWN: Mine the forest to save the forest. Like: let's make friends with Afghanistan by dropping bombs on them.
HARRY: And what have you ever done for 'the environment'? Really? Dumping shit on the rest of us from your professorial chair.
DIXON-BROWN: Ha. Nothing so high and mighty, I'm just like any other head of department—forced to sell out to any sleazebag who walks through the door with a fat wad of cash.
HARRY: Dix.
DIXON-BROWN: You're a con man, Harry. Congratulations. I fell for it.
HARRY: Fine.

He exits to the bedroom to get his clothes.

DIXON-BROWN *checks her email on her phone.*

DIXON-BROWN: Oh, my God.
HARRY: What?
DIXON-BROWN: Oh, my God.
HARRY: What is it?

Beat.

Dix?

HARRY *appears half-dressed.*

DIXON-BROWN: Somebody has sent an email to all staff in our faculty.
'The CAPE Institute, headed by Professor Dixon-Brown, receives substantial research funding from Powerhouse Mining. The company's Chief Executive Officer, Harry Jewell, is having a covert sexual relationship with Dixon-Brown ... She failed to show due diligence ... jeopardising public trust ... The Board of Powerhouse will shortly act to remove Mr Jewell and charge him with misappropriation of company funds.'

HARRY: Bullshit. Who sent that?
DIXON-BROWN: Is it your money to give?
HARRY: Of course it bloody is. It's my company.
DIXON-BROWN: It's a public company.
HARRY: Which I founded. Which I run. In which I am the largest shareholder. Who sent that?
DIXON-BROWN: I don't know.
HARRY: Andy.
DIXON-BROWN: Andy?
HARRY: When was it sent?

 Beat.

Dix?
DIXON-BROWN: Two minutes ago.
HARRY: Andy.
DIXON-BROWN: Andy would never do something like this.
HARRY: On account of being such a hero.
DIXON-BROWN: Oh, gawd.
HARRY: Your brother is a fanatic. He would betray his own sister. For what? It's not going to stop us mining coal.

SCENE FOUR

Dixon-Brown's office.

DIXON-BROWN *is working on her computer. There is a knock at the door.*

DIXON-BROWN: Come in.

 PIPER *enters.*

PIPER: You wanted to see me?
DIXON-BROWN: Do you know where Andy is?
PIPER: No.
DIXON-BROWN: He's not answering his phone.
PIPER: Is something wrong?
DIXON-BROWN: No.

 What about you? Everything going along okay?
PIPER: Yes. Fine.

 I know this is really bad timing, but I thought maybe I should take a couple of weeks off and go visit my mom.

DIXON-BROWN: Your mum, or your dog?

PIPER: Well ... both. I was thinking of leaving next week and when I get back I could start full time on the Powerhouse project.

DIXON-BROWN: Let me tell you something that will clarify your situation here. Last night someone—I don't know who—circulated an email to every member of staff at the university. It described a threat to the reputation of the university because a member of staff was having a covert sexual relationship with Harry Jewell.

PIPER is horrified.

PIPER: Did it name the member of staff?

DIXON-BROWN: Yes.

Beat.

I did something very unethical. And I trust you will not repeat this to a single soul. I came in, in the middle of the night, with the head of IT and we deleted the email from the system.

PIPER: So nobody read it.

DIXON-BROWN: Hopefully not.

PIPER: Oh, Dix.

Thank you.

DIXON-BROWN: It's okay.

PIPER: I was going to tell you. I was. I knew it was a mistake. I've been such an idiot. I knew it would compromise the whole integrity of the project. I'm so sorry. I don't know what I was thinking.

DIXON-BROWN: You were charmed by Harry Jewell.

PIPER: Who sent the email?

DIXON-BROWN: Someone who doesn't like us. But to be perfectly frank with you, I don't think this is the end of it.

PIPER: What happens now?

DIXON-BROWN: You'll need to step aside from the project.

PIPER: Oh, no.

DIXON-BROWN: I've had a conversation with the San Diego Zoo. They're keen to get you back.

PIPER: I see.

DIXON-BROWN: Since it's over between you and Andy, there's not a lot keeping you here.

There is a knock at the door. HARRY *enters.*

HARRY: Piper?
DIXON-BROWN: What's up?
HARRY: The board has just sacked me.
DIXON-BROWN: Harry.
HARRY: They had an emergency meeting. Clovis Carter moved that the project was an inappropriate use of company funds citing 'gross misconduct'.
DIXON-BROWN: What for?
HARRY: It gets better. Clovis rang me before the meeting, urging me to resign. He said if I refused, he'd urge the board to press criminal charges.
DIXON-BROWN: Criminal charges!? What the hell for?
HARRY: He claims I misrepresented the project as an environmental impact study connected to mining in the forest. Which he's pushing for, of course.
DIXON-BROWN: Is that what you did?
HARRY: No. I represented it as a public relations exercise. Which they bought. But the fact is, I am the only one standing between them and the forest.
DIXON-BROWN: Shit.
HARRY: Then, thanks to Andy, they get this email.
PIPER: What's Andy got to do with it?
DIXON-BROWN: Nothing.
HARRY: Oh, how wrong you are. The chairman of my board gets an email from someone saying that I am embezzling their money.
PIPER: What? Is that the same email?
DIXON-BROWN: No.
PIPER: Do you know about this, Harry? Someone sent an email to staff at the university saying you and I are having an affair.
HARRY: You and I?

He glances at DIXON-BROWN.

Which we're not!
PIPER: It's okay. She knows.

Beat.

DIXON-BROWN: What did the email to your chairman say?

HARRY: It said that you and I were having a covert sexual relationship—
DIXON-BROWN: Which we're not!
HARRY: It was just sex.
DIXON-BROWN: Oh, for godsake.
PIPER: You two had sex?
DIXON-BROWN: Once.
HARRY: Twice. Maybe ten times. I'm sorry, Piper.
PIPER: You had sex with *him*!?
DIXON-BROWN: It was a long time ago.
HARRY: It was last night. Which is *why* Andy distributed those emails. He came to the apartment, saw my car out the front, and two minutes later he sprayed his emails to all and sundry. Destroying the project and clearing the way for Powerhouse to mine in the forest. Great work. He's a great guy. Confirming everything you might think about 'environmentalists'—what utter naive dickheads they are.

HARRY stands.

DIXON-BROWN: Harry? Where are you going?
HARRY: Where d'you think?

HARRY exits.

DIXON-BROWN: Andy's place.

DIXON-BROWN jumps up and grabs her coat. She exits.

PIPER is left alone. She grabs her stuff and runs after them.

SCENE FIVE

The animal shelter.

Lights up on ANDY. *He is placing two books in the bookcase when the bell dings in reception.* HARRY *barges in. He is in a fury.*

ANDY: Oi!
HARRY: You piece of shit.

HARRY is carrying a rolled ordinance map. He lays it out on the table where he and Piper examined the quoll. He switches the light on.

ANDY: What the fuck are you doing? Piss off.

HARRY *takes the books out of* ANDY's *hands to hold down the map.*

HARRY: You've really screwed up this time.

ANDY: Out. Get. Out.

HARRY: She's your own sister. That's what I can't understand.

ANDY: What are you talking about?

HARRY *thumps his finger on the map.*

HARRY: This is where the board of Powerhouse had a permit to explore for coal. Forest. Right on the edge of the national park.

But I persuaded them, after months of sweet-talking, to shift here. Sixty k's west.

No forest. Done deal.

Till you blunder in.

ANDY: Me?

HARRY: You gave them the go-ahead to get rid of the man—the *one* man—standing between them and the forest. Can you hear the trees falling out there, Andy?

ANDY: You've got the wrong end of the stick, mate.

HARRY: Thirty million bucks. That's what this forest is worth to Clovis Carter and his mates.

ANDY: Harry?

HARRY: You think they're gonna walk away from that? And then! All their Christmases come at once.

ANDY: I don't know what you're talking about.

HARRY: You handed them the forest on a plate. Cousin Country Andy shoots off his pathetic emails.

ANDY: What emails?

HARRY: Yeah, right.

ANDY: Harry. I don't know shit about any email.

HARRY: Clean coal. It's the only way forward, Andy.

ANDY: What part of this do you not understand?

HARRY: It's the cheapest, most abundant fuel on the planet.

ANDY: It's the absolute dirtiest.

HARRY: And it's booming worldwide. / Sorry to have to tell you.

ANDY: [*ticking off the problems*] Toxic waste; acid rain; air pollution /

HARRY: / But we can change the way we use it.

We're investing massive amounts of money—

ANDY: In bullshit. In lies and bullshit.
HARRY: This was gonna make a difference. A real difference.
ANDY: If you cared one jot for that country out there [*pointing out the window*] you'd put your money into wind power.
HARRY: Solar, wind: I can't tell you how much I would like them to be the answer.
ANDY: But your hands are tied. I understand. You make an obscene amount of money—
HARRY: Renewables are never going to generate all your baseload power.
ANDY: People like you talk like you're the future. But you're the old world. Old privilege. Old money. Old greed.
HARRY: You don't know anything about me.

Beat.

Your wife runs off with your best mate.

You hit some innocent creature—

You want your whole life to be different. Stand for something.

ANDY: Well, stand for something, then.
HARRY: What do you think I've been doing? What do you think this was all about?
ANDY: I've got no idea, mate. You're the only one who knows the answer to that.

DIXON-BROWN *rushes in.*

DIXON-BROWN: [*to* ANDY] Are you alright? I thought he was going to kill you.
ANDY: As if.

Maybe silence?

DIXON-BROWN: I had a call from our IT department. They've traced the email.
ANDY: What friggin' email??
DIXON-BROWN: It was your wife.
HARRY: My wife?
DIXON-BROWN: Stephanie.
HARRY: What?
DIXON-BROWN: Your wife is Stephanie Jewell. Is she not? She emailed every single staff member in the science faculty.

HARRY *is trying to take this in. He is devastated. He nods.*

HARRY: Stephanie sent that email? How? How did she do that?
DIXON-BROWN: Everyone's address is on the university website.
HARRY: Wow. Why would she do that?
DIXON-BROWN: She hates you. You seem to have this effect on women.
HARRY: Are they gonna sack you?
DIXON-BROWN: Don't be ridiculous. I rang Alan Dodd.
HARRY: The IT guy?
DIXON-BROWN: I rang him immediately after you left last night.
HARRY: Like one o'clock in the morning?
DIXON-BROWN: One-thirty. I told him we had an emergency. And he had to meet me at the IT department.
ANDY: At half-past one in the morning?
HARRY: Did it work?
DIXON-BROWN: Turns out, it's pretty simple. He deleted the email from everyone's mailbox.
ANDY: And he can just do that?
DIXON-BROWN: Not without authority.
HARRY: But what if someone's read it already? The cat's out of the bag.
DIXON-BROWN: Harry, it's sorted. No-one has read it. Just me.
HARRY: So, you're off the hook?
ANDY: You have no shame.
HARRY: She has no shame.
ANDY: What about Piper?
HARRY: What's it to you?
ANDY: She's my girlfriend.
HARRY: You lost that race a long time ago.
ANDY: Meaning?

Long pause.

DIXON-BROWN: [*to* HARRY] You need to come with me, now.

HARRY *makes to exit through reception.* DIXON-BROWN *directs him out through the other door.*

This way.
Andy, Piper is in reception.
HARRY: You shouldn't have let her go, mate.

They exit.

ANDY *goes to the door. He pauses. He opens the door. He stands there.*

ANDY: Next?

PIPER *enters. There is an awkwardness between them.*

Mate.

PIPER: I've just come to say goodbye. I'm going back to the States. On the weekend.

ANDY: For good?

PIPER *shrugs.*

Back to the zoo?

PIPER: Via New York. See my mom.

ANDY: Started eating yet?

PIPER: Just the corn chips.

ANDY: Still the barbecue flavour?

PIPER: Cheese Supreme.

How's Bluey Nicholls' dog?

ANDY: I had to put him down.

PIPER: Poor old Bluey.

So. Are you going to sell the practice? Move to El Salvador?

ANDY: I'm sick.

PIPER: What?

ANDY: I have GSS. It's a disease.

PIPER: GSS?

ANDY: It's a brain disorder. My grandfather had it. Worse luck for me, it runs in our family.

PIPER: I've never heard of it.

ANDY: It's a bit like Parkinson's. Except … it gets you when you're forty.

PIPER: How do you know you've got this thing? I mean, are you sure?

ANDY: I've had the test.

PIPER: What's the—?

ANDY: The prognosis? Six years. That's the average.

PIPER: Does Dix know?

ANDY: She's my sister.

PIPER: Why didn't you tell me?

ANDY: I only just found out.
PIPER: You just had the test?
ANDY: No. I … I had the test when I was a kid. The truth is, it's only just started to show itself.
PIPER: But you've known for a long time?
ANDY: Since I was thirteen.
PIPER: And you never once wanted to tell me?
ANDY: I never once wanted to live my life as a dying man.
PIPER: We've been together for two years.
ANDY: I'm sorry.
PIPER: I'm not leaving.
ANDY: Yes, you are.
PIPER: No—
ANDY: You're going to the airport on the weekend.
PIPER: —I'm not.
ANDY: You don't need to prove to yourself that you're a good person.
PIPER: No, I don't. But you can't face this on your own.
ANDY: I've been facing it all my life.
PIPER: What will happen to you?
ANDY: You don't want to know.
PIPER: I do. I want to know. You can't keep this from me.
ANDY: Piper. Calm down.
PIPER: No. I can't. This is not fair. We've only just got started.
ANDY: And this is where it ends. You can't be a part of this.
PIPER: I won't be pushed away. I won't.
ANDY: Mate, you're a traveller. You're passing through.

He turns away.

PIPER: We're all just passing through.
ANDY: I don't want to look into your eyes and see pity.
PIPER: I have a pain in here [*her chest*] that you could think of facing this without me.
ANDY: This road, Piper …
PIPER: This road?
ANDY: It just leads to sadness.

She looks out the window.

PIPER: Do you still not believe there are any tiger quolls out there?

ANDY: I'm the bloke who killed the last one. Remember?

PIPER's phone beeps. She looks down.

PIPER: Andy. Look.

On the monitor on the back wall, the camera catches a small creature staring into the frame. Its nose twitches. Its black eyes gleam. It is a tiger quoll. Its heart is beating.

THE END

Marta Kaczmarek (left) as Joan and Eva Seymour as Melissa in Red Stitch Actors Theatre's 2016 production of The Honey Bees. *(Photo: Jodie Hutchinson)*

THE HONEY BEES

Caleb Lewis

CALEB LEWIS is a multi-award-winning writer for the stage.

Graduating with first class honours from Flinders University, Lewis was mentored by both Nick Enright and Edward Albee. His plays have been shortlisted for the Western Australian Premier's Award; the Griffin Award (twice); and have won an Inscription Award, the Mitch Mathews Award and the inaugural Australian Writers' Guild Award for Digital Narrative. His play, *Clinchfield*, is the inaugural winner of the Richard Burton Award for New Plays. Caleb's work has been commissioned and/or produced by Bell Shakespeare (NSW); Black Swan State Theatre Company (WA); State Theatre Company of South Australia; Hothouse (Vic); and numerous companies across the country.

His plays include *Nailed*; *Men, Love and the Monkeyboy*; *Dogfall*; *Death in Bowengabbie*, *Rust and Bone*; *Aleksander and the Robot Maid*; *Clinchfield*; *Tribute*; *Destroyer of Worlds*; *Six Million Hits*; and *Maggie Stone* (published by Currency Press).

Caleb is currently writer in residence with Melbourne's Red Stitch Actors Theatre. He is studying Video Game Narrative through the University of British Columbia and completing a residency with Blast Theory (UK). He was recently named by Flinders University as a Top 50 Creative Alumnus.

The Honey Bees was first produced at Red Stitch Actors Theatre, St Kilda, on 14 June 2016, with the following cast:

JOAN	Marta Kaczmarek
DARYL	Christopher Brown
CLOVER	Rebecca Bower
KERRIE	Katerina Kotsonis
MELISSA	Eva Seymour

Director, Ella Caldwell
Set Designer, Michael Hankin
Dramaturg, Tom Healey
Set & Costume Designer, Sophie Woodward
Lighting Designer, Daniel Anderson
Sound Designer, Daniel Nixon
Stage Manager, Hannah Bullen
Assistant Stage Manager, Madison Lyman

'In 2008 more food was grown than ever before in history. In 2008 more people were obese than ever before in history. In 2008 more profit was made by food companies than ever before in history. And in 2008 more people went hungry than ever before in history.'

Eric Holt-Giménez

'Our economic system and our planetary system are now at war ... What the climate needs to avoid collapse is a contraction in humanity's use of resources; what our economic model demands to avoid collapse is unfettered expansion.'

Naomi Klein

'And God said unto them, Be fruitful, and multiply, and replenish the earth, and subdue it: and have dominion over the fish of the sea, and over the fowl of the air, and over every living thing that moveth upon the earth.'

Genesis 1:28

WRITER'S NOTE

The Honey Bees began with two questions:

What is the endpoint of our relentless growth? And what happens to us if the bees disappear?

The much-lauded agricultural innovations of the Green Revolution (1930s–1960s) served to industrialise production and feed millions—but with an overreliance on pesticides, fertilisers, GM crops and monoculture, does this miracle panacea come at too high a cost?

The Honey Bees is a play about economics and our relationship with the natural world. As the last remaining country yet unaffected by Colony Collapse Disorder—a phenomenon that has decimated the world's bees—Australia's position is unique. Can we learn from the mistakes of others? Or are we doomed to repeat them?

In late June 2016, during the run of *The Honey Bees* in Melbourne, varroa mites were detected in a nest of honey bees in Townsville. Despite our best efforts, Trevor Weatherhead, Executive Director of the Australian Honeybee Industry Council, acknowledged that the mite could decimate Australia's honey bees.

Thank you to Ella Caldwell and all at Red Stitch Actors Theatre for championing this new Australian work and bringing it to the stage with the help of a magnificent cast and crew. I am indebted to Sally Burton and Onward Productions for commissioning the play and also to Chris Mead, Tim Roseman, Tom Healey and Tom Holloway for their input on the script. Special thanks to Jane Bodie, Iain Sinclair, Lawrie Cullen-Tait, Alex Vickery-Howe, Peta Hanrahan and the many others who generously gave their time and expertise in guiding this work to the stage. Thanks to Anna and Andrew at Honeycomb Valley for introducing me to the world of bees and to Alf and Anna at Upper Beaconsfield Apiary for their feedback and professional expertise. Lastly, a huge thanks to Suzie Miller, whose conviction for this project never wavered. *The Honey Bees* would not exist without her insight and support.

Caleb Lewis

CHARACTERS

JOAN, 60s, a widow, matriarch of the 'Uncle Harry's' brand
DARYL, early 40s, Joan's son
CLOVER (CLO), late 30s, Joan's daughter
KERRIE, early 50s, Joan's leading hand, Clo's partner
MELISSA, early 20s, a car crash, an outsider

A NOTE ON THE STAGING

The play takes place on an Australian-run apiary, expanding into the live export of bees to America in 2009.

The set consists of a number of old wooden hive boxes, faded and sun-starched. Once-bright paint flakes away. Some are stacked like tombstones; others lie at strange angles like jagged teeth.

Every box drips with honey: thick amber fluid that sweats from cracks and joists and drips down the walls, staining everything.

The hive boxes are covered with tablecloths and linen to make up the set. There is a sense of denial here. Of history unchallenged.

Joan's hives (for the sale) are plain and unadorned. Clo's hives (producing 'Uncle Harry's Honey') are painted in bright colours, resembling Cinque Terre on the Italian coast. These hives may not at first be visible to the audience.

/   A slash indicates the next speech begins at that point.
-     A dash indicates the next line interrupts/cuts off at this point.
…   An ellipsis at the end of a speech indicates it trails off.
…   A lone ellipsis indicates an expectation or desire to speak.
( )   A bracketed phrase is considered but remains unspoken.

SCENE ONE

Darkness.
The drone of crickets; the endless buzz of bees.
A warm background hum that will continue throughout most of the play.
...
Then ...
Sounds of a car approaching, speeding, engine roaring.
Rock music. Almost deafening.
Screech of tyres.
Impact!
Sudden blast of a car horn, sustained.
The bees become agitated, their buzzing grows louder and LOUDER.
Pandemonium. Chaos.

SCENE TWO

The verandah.
Outside, the endless hum of bees.
DARYL, *in suit and tie, overnight bag by his feet.* JOAN *sits, hive tool in hand, working propolis off a frame.*
Eventually ...

JOAN: There's a hive tool on the table.

    Beat.

    DARYL *takes up a frame and a hive tool.*

    JOAN *watches him.*

  You remember how?
DARYL: 'Course.
JOAN: Not so hard. You only need to tap it. / Don't—
DARYL: I know.

    JOAN *sighs.*

Beat.

Where is everyone?

JOAN: Working.

A bee circles lazily overhead. DARYL *tenses.* JOAN *watches him. She finishes her frame.*

DARYL: Can we go inside?

JOAN: I'm not finished yet.

JOAN *picks up another.*

Beat.

DARYL: Had a look at the eucalypts driving down. Not a lot flowering … You must be driving up to Broome and back chasing the honey flow.

JOAN: More like a drip.

DARYL: I can't believe you've done it. All these years on your own.

CLO *enters.*

CLO: Cup of / tea, Mum.

DARYL *slips the hive tool and strikes his own thumb.*

DARYL: Fuck!

He sticks his thumb in his mouth, chucks the hive tool in anger.

JOAN *sighs, continues working.*

JOAN: Look who's all grown-up.

DARYL *stands, still sucking his thumb. Stops.*

DARYL: Didn't think I'd miss the sale?

Beat.

CLO: I'll set another place for tea.

JOAN: Get him a plaster.

DARYL: I'm fine.

CLO: Come on.

She heads inside the house. DARYL *follows.*

Once inside …

How long'd she keep you out there?

DARYL: Not long.

CLO: I think there's some bandaids in the—
  What?
DARYL: The house. It looks exactly—
CLO: Like a mausoleum?
DARYL: Nothing's changed. Even the wallpaper.
CLO: We got aircon.
DARYL: … It's good to see you, Clo.
CLO: Is it?
DARYL: You haven't changed a bit.

She hands him a plaster.

Thanks.
CLO: What are you doing here?
DARYL: Can't I visit?
CLO: Don't you trust us?
DARYL: I just wanted to be here.
CLO: Why?
DARYL: To see them loaded up.
CLO: From inside?

DARYL puts the plaster on.

DARYL: How's Kez?
CLO: You can ask her.
DARYL: She back?
CLO: Tonight.
DARYL: And that's the last of them?
CLO: All five hundred hives.
DARYL: Five?
CLO: It's been a shitty season.
DARYL: But that's not what we / promised.
CLO: I don't control the weather.
DARYL: The deal's six hundred.
CLO: It hasn't rained for months. / And with the drought there's less flowering—
DARYL: Okay, I get that. But—
  Jesus, why didn't anyone tell me?
CLO: Daryl, that's thirty million bees.
DARYL: Twenty-five million.

CLO: [*rhetorically*] What are you gonna do?
DARYL: How many have you got?
CLO: No.
DARYL: A hundred and fifty hives?
CLO: You're not having them.
DARYL: I'm doing this for us!
CLO: Get your own bees.

    CLO *rises, exits.*

DARYL: [*calling after her*] This thing is a gold rush! And when you and Mum are set for life! Then maybe you'll thank me!

    CLO *re-enters.*

CLO: If this fucks up, it's on you.

    JOAN *enters.*

JOAN: What's wrong?
CLO: The woofers quit.
JOAN: When?!
CLO: An hour ago.
JOAN: And when were you gonna tell me?!
CLO: I'm telling you now.
JOAN: Laziness.
CLO: They were hard workers, Mum.
JOAN: Not hard enough.
CLO: For eight bucks an hour?
JOAN: Plus food and board.
CLO: In a tent. And you're out there waking them at four every morning.
JOAN: So?
CLO: What do you expect?
JOAN: Loyalty.

    Beat.

CLO: Well, now there's just us.

    Beat.

DARYL: Is there anything I can do?
JOAN: [*ignoring him*] What time's Kez due?
CLO: She left Geraldton just after ten.

JOAN: Is everything ready?
CLO: No.
JOAN: How are they?
CLO: Hungry.
JOAN: Don't start—
CLO: They've already foraged everything close by.
DARYL: So they can fly a little further.
CLO: They're exhausted.
DARYL: Don't they have honey?
CLO: We already took it to make room for more brood.
DARYL: So supp them with sugar.
CLO: Thanks for the tip!
DARYL: Do you want them to starve?
CLO: They're already crowded. And now you're bringing in more.
DARYL: It's one night.
CLO: It's reckless.
JOAN: We've been through this.
CLO: Hundreds of hives from all over the state and now you're throwing them all together / and crossing your fingers—
JOAN: Twenty-four hours.
 We house them here for one night, then tomorrow load up the last of the hives on the truck, drive to Sydney, get the bees on the plane. And then we're done.
CLO: If nothing goes wrong.
DARYL: It won't.
CLO: If Dad were here—
JOAN: Well, he's *not*.
CLO: We don't have to do this.
DARYL: It's done.
CLO: The honey's good. And people are still buying it.
DARYL: What are you talking / about?
JOAN: Both of you, that's enough! Clover, I've heard all your arguments. And I've made my decision. Make no mistake, this deal is going / ahead—

The door bursts open and KERRIE *enters with* MELISSA *in her arms, unconscious.*

CLO: Kerrie?
KERRIE: Give us a hand, will ya.
JOAN: What happened?
KERRIE: Take her legs.
DARYL: Who is she?
KERRIE: Help me get her down.
JOAN: Where'd she come from?
KERRIE: Found her out by the road.
JOAN: Where?
KERRIE: Crashed into the hives.
JOAN: The bees?
CLO: Mum!
KERRIE: She must have veered off the road.
JOAN: And the bees?
KERRIE: At least forty hives.
DARYL: Forty?!

From left: Marta Kaczmarek as Joan, Eva Seymour (lying) as Melissa, Rebecca Bower as Clover, Katerina Kotsonis as Kerrie and Christopher Brown as Daryl in Red Stitch Actors Theatre's 2016 production of THE HONEY BEES. (Photo: Jodie Hutchinson)

KERRIE: Nothing left but splinters.
CLO: Who is she?
KERRIE: They were there in the car with her. Thousands of them. I thought she was a goner.
CLO: I'll get the epipen.
KERRIE: There's no stings.
JOAN: What?
CLO: None.
DARYL: Mum?
JOAN: ... Put her in the den.

SCENE THREE

Thursday night. Home. Lights out.

DARYL *is on the couch on his laptop, with dongle and headphones.*

DARYL: [*on the phone*] Mate? Let me tell you, Hank, I was out there today. You should see these bees. If they were any healthier, they'd tow the plane there themselves.
   Great—
   There is one thing. Not a big deal. Only we're a little bit under ...
   No, it's not a joke.
   The minimum, I know.

   He holds the phone away.

Hank? Hank? Can I—?
   Will you just let me. Listen!
   ...
   Gotcha!
   Six hundred hives. As promised.
   And then the next batch in three m—

   MELISSA *enters in an oversized shirt. She stumbles, knocks something over.*

MELISSA: [*under her breath*] Fuck.

   DARYL *hears her.*

DARYL: [*winding up the call*] Mmhm.
   Yep.

I'll call you once they're on the truck.
Bonzer!

He hangs up.

[*To* MELISSA] Hey?

MELISSA: Water.

DARYL *points to the kitchen.* MELISSA *stumbles offstage. Sounds of a tap running.*

Beat.

The tap switches off. Silence.

DARYL: Hello?

He closes the laptop, rises.

MELISSA *enters with a glass of water. She takes his seat on the couch, head in hands.*

How you feeling?

MELISSA *holds her hand up to quiet him. She gulps down the water. He waits. She puts down the glass.*

MELISSA: More.

Beat.

DARYL *takes her glass. Exits.*

The sound of a tap running.

He re-enters with a full glass. She takes it without thanks. Gulps it down then ...

Time is it?

DARYL: Late.

Beat.

I'm Daryl.

MELISSA: [*with a laugh*] 'Daryl'.

DARYL: You don't remember how you got here?

MELISSA: ...

DARYL: You had a bit to drink.

MELISSA *raises her eyebrows.*

Oh. We didn't—you were passed out.

MELISSA: You shoulda had a crack.

DARYL: You've been in an accident.

> MELISSA *remembering, panicked, starts to check herself for bees or stings.*

They didn't sting you. We checked. My sister. She used to be a nurse.

Beat.

MELISSA: …

DARYL: What's your name?

MELISSA: … Melissa.

DARYL: Is there someone we can call?

MELISSA: Like who?

DARYL: They might be looking for you?

MELISSA: The cops?

DARYL: Your mum and dad.

> MELISSA *laughs.*

Someone else then?

MELISSA: …

DARYL: Are you hungry? I think there's—

MELISSA: Where are we?

DARYL: Darradup.

MELISSA: Darradup?

DARYL: You know it?

MELISSA: What is this place?

DARYL: Welcome to Honeycomb Creek.

MELISSA: …

DARYL: Mel? Are you alright?

MELISSA: Melissa.

DARYL: Ever heard of Uncle Harry?

MELISSA: Who?

DARYL: Uncle Harry.

MELISSA: Sounds like a paedophile.

DARYL: Uncle Harry's Honey. It's a brand name. Used to be in supermarkets. 'Uncle Harry's / Honey'?

MELISSA: Stop saying it.

DARYL: Sorry.
MELISSA: The guy on radio?
DARYL: That's him.
MELISSA: 'What's the buzz?'
DARYL: That's my dad.
MELISSA: Your dad? So you're …
DARYL: Harry Junior!
MELISSA: I thought it was Daryl.
DARYL: It is.
MELISSA: But he's dead, right?
DARYL: Yeah. He is.
MELISSA: When?
DARYL: A few years back.
MELISSA: How did he—?
DARYL: Heart attack.

Beat.

Lucky you were wearing your seatbelt. Kez said it looked like you drove straight into them.
MELISSA: This your shirt?

MELISSA *starts to take it off.*

DARYL: Stop! It's one of Clo's. Keep it, it's yours.

MELISSA *shrugs, leaves it on.*

Beat.

Do you remember anything?
MELISSA: …
DARYL: Melissa?
MELISSA: [*changing the subject*] 'Bonzer'?
DARYL: Oh. You heard that?
MELISSA: What was that about?
DARYL: He's American.
MELISSA: Crikey!
DARYL: We're selling them bees.
MELISSA: I thought you sold honey?
DARYL: We did. I mean we do.

MELISSA: How many?
DARYL: Five hundred. Hives. Minus the ones you took out.
MELISSA: Sorry.
DARYL: It's fine. [*It's not.*]
MELISSA: What's wrong with their bees?
DARYL: They're sick.
MELISSA: What's wrong with them?
DARYL: It doesn't matter. The point is there's money to be made.
MELISSA: What'll happen to them? The bees. Once they get there.
DARYL: They die. Or abandon the hives like the others. And then the Yanks buy more.
MELISSA: For how long?
DARYL: As long as it lasts.
MELISSA: You said six hundred.
DARYL: What?
MELISSA: Not five hundred. Hives.
DARYL: Did I?
MELISSA: Better get onto that.

> MELISSA *gets up to leave.*

DARYL: Where are you going?
MELISSA: Where's my stuff?
DARYL: On the chair.

> MELISSA *exits.*

> DARYL *waits a moment.*

> MELISSA *re-enters.*

MELISSA: Thanks for the shirt.
DARYL: What are you doing?

> *He stands.*

It's the middle of the night!
MELISSA: Just tell me where the car is and I'll—
DARYL: Up the road.
MELISSA: Thanks.
DARYL: Wrapped around a tree.

> *That stops her.*

Look, no one's going anywhere tonight. Just stay till morning. We'll figure all of this out then.

MELISSA *nods*.

SCENE FOUR

Friday morning. Early. Before dawn. The kitchen.

KERRIE *sits as* CLO *massages her back. There's nothing gentle about it.*

CLO: Of all the fucking days!

MELISSA *enters, unseen, in t-shirt and knickers. She watches them.*

KERRIE: I'll be fine.
CLO: Ha!
KERRIE: A bit of Deep Heat.
CLO: You can barely—
KERRIE: What was I supposed to do? Leave her?
CLO: I'm not blaming you.
KERRIE: It sounds like it.
CLO: Mum's gonna have a fit.
KERRIE: They were all over her. I thought they'd kill her for sure.
CLO: Well, now we're fucked.
MELISSA: [*interrupting*] Where's the toilet?
CLO: Oh.
KERRIE: Morning.
CLO: You gave us a scare last night.
MELISSA: I'm busting.

CLO *points offstage.* MELISSA *exits.*

A raised eyebrow between CLO *and* KERRIE.

CLO: Shoulda left her in the car.

JOAN *enters.*

JOAN: Ready?

KERRIE *rises, winces.*

What's wrong?
KERRIE: Nothing.
CLO: Her back.

KERRIE: Just a twinge.
CLO: It's stuffed.
JOAN: Can you work?
KERRIE: / Yes—
CLO: No.
JOAN: The truck leaves tonight.

> DARYL *wanders in.*

Lindsay Lohan up?
DARYL: Who?
JOAN: Twinkle-tits. The girl.
CLO: Bathroom.
DARYL: Any coffee left?
JOAN: Who is she?

> MELISSA *enters.*

DARYL: Ah, Mum, this is Mel … lissa.
JOAN: How you feeling?
MELISSA: Got any Panadol?
JOAN: Clo.

> CLO *exits to the bathroom.*

[*To* KERRIE] Bring the truck round out back.

> KERRIE *exits outside.*

> DARYL *sits.*

Give Kez a hand.
DARYL: Outside?
JOAN: Give me strength.
DARYL: I have to make call.

> DARYL *exits.*

> CLO *enters, slams the Panadol down on the table, exits.*

> JOAN, *nonplussed, sits regarding* MELISSA.

JOAN: Well, aren't you a cutey? Bet it gets you into all sorts of strife.
MELISSA: …
JOAN: Where you from?
MELISSA: Around.

JOAN: Not around here.
MELISSA: …
JOAN: How'd you get here?
MELISSA: Just the wrong crowd, I guess.
JOAN: Want to tell me what you were doing last night?
MELISSA: Speed. I think. Oh, and a bottle of Jack. And some pills as well.
JOAN: You cost me forty good hives.
MELISSA: …
JOAN: Those bees out there—
The ones you ram-raided. You know how much they're worth?
MELISSA: So don't leave them by the side of the road.
JOAN: If you'd stayed on the road—
MELISSA: I could have died!
JOAN: And why didn't you?! Bees seething around you fit to black out the sky and look at you, not a sting to be seen …
MELISSA: …
JOAN: How's your neck?
MELISSA: My neck?
JOAN: Any whiplash?
MELISSA: Look. I'm not gonna sue.
JOAN: That's funny.

JOAN reaches for the phone.

MELISSA: What are you doing?
JOAN: Calling the police.
MELISSA: Stop.

Beat.

JOAN: A record, hey?
MELISSA: What do you want?
JOAN: What would you want?
MELISSA: An apology?
JOAN: That's cute.
MELISSA: Hang up.
JOAN: Licence?
MELISSA: I don't have one. I mean I lost it.
JOAN: I'm shocked.
MELISSA: Can't we figure something out?

Please?

JOAN *puts the phone down. Waits.*

I don't have any money.

JOAN: I need workers.

We're five men down and thanks to your cunning little stunt my lead hand is a gimp.

I've got one hundred and sixty hives out there need loading up with the rest. But looking at you ... You ever done a hard day's work in your life?

MELISSA: And you won't call the cops?

JOAN *rises, leaves the room.*

MELISSA *waits.*

JOAN *re-enters with a jar filled with trapped bees. She sets it down on the table.*

What are they?

JOAN *opens the jar, covers the lid with her hand.*

Hello?

JOAN: Put your arm out.

MELISSA: Why?

JOAN: Back in Poland. In my village. When a couple got engaged, they had a test. The girl had to walk through a corridor of beehives. And if she got stung, well she must be a tart.

Take you. Drinking like a trollop, getting about in your knickers. Some people might call you a slut.

But. If we were back in Poland, you'd say, 'Ask the bees. I'm as pure as the driven snow.'

JOAN *opens the jar, reaches inside.*

MELISSA: What are you doing?

JOAN: Shhh, Mumma only needs one of you.

She pinches a bee between her fingers.

There.

MELISSA: What are you—?

JOAN: Hold still.

MELISSA: Fuck off.
JOAN: You want to work here?
MELISSA: Not that much.
JOAN: Fine.

> JOAN *reaches for the phone.*

MELISSA: Don't!
JOAN: If you're allergic, I can't use you.
MELISSA: I'll wear a bee costume.
JOAN: How tall are you?
MELISSA: Five-four.
JOAN: You don't think they'll catch on?
MELISSA: A bee suit. You know what I mean.
JOAN: It's forty degrees out there.
MELISSA: Wait!
JOAN: You know what anaphylaxis is? If you want to work here, I need to know you're not gonna go into shock and die on me the minute you get stung.
MELISSA: But last night.
JOAN: You were lucky.
MELISSA: But—
JOAN: Roll up your sleeve.

> *Beat.* MELISSA *does so.*
>
> JOAN *takes the bee out and kisses it.*

[*To the bee*] Thank you.

> JOAN *holds it over* MELISSA*'s wrist.*

Now ...
MELISSA: Is it gonna hurt?
JOAN: What do you think?

> JOAN *holds the bee down. It stings.*

MELISSA: *Faaaaaaaaaarrrrrrrkkkkk!*
JOAN: Give me your arm.
MELISSA: Fuck. Off.
JOAN: Now.

> MELISSA *holds her arm out.* JOAN *flicks the bee off.*

Hold still.

MELISSA: Aw, fuck it hurts.

> JOAN, *unhurried, scrapes the stinger out.*

JOAN: There. We'll keep an eye on you for the next half an hour and if there's no reaction I'll put you to work.

MELISSA: Aren't you gonna put anything on it?

> JOAN *spits.*

Hey!

> JOAN *rubs it into her arm.*

JOAN: Best thing for it.

SCENE FIVE

Friday mid-morning. The hives.

CLO *and* MELISSA *are out among the hives.*

MELISSA: Don't I need protection?
CLO: It's a beehive, not a brothel.
MELISSA: What if I get bit again?
CLO: Stung.
MELISSA: Whatever.

> CLO *throws her a bundled outfit.*

CLO: Put this on.
MELISSA: I'll be right.
CLO: You weren't worried about it last night.
MELISSA: I was off my tits!

> MELISSA *sighs, starts getting dressed.*

CLO: Hurry up. You're worse than a woofer.
MELISSA: Chill out.
CLO: I hate this.
MELISSA: [*smartarse*] Don't you like the bees?
CLO: Not this many.
MELISSA: What's a woofer?
CLO: Backpacker.
MELISSA: Oh.

CLO: Tuck your socks in.

> MELISSA *does so.*

And the hood.

MELISSA: Why can't Daryl help?

CLO: Ask him.

> *She takes a smoker out, stuffs it with a handful of pine needles. She sets them alight, working the bellows a few times till the flame takes hold.* MELISSA *finishes getting dressed.*
>
> CLO *zips her up. Pats her on the back—she's done.*

Let's go.

> *They cross the stage.*

See this?

> CLO *works the bellows a few times, jetting out puffs of smoke.*

Here.

> *She passes* MELISSA *the smoker.*

MELISSA: What is it?

CLO: See those hives over there?

MELISSA: Yeah.

CLO: Give 'em three or four puffs.

> MELISSA *does so. She gives another couple for good measure.*

Righto, it's not a blue light disco.

> *A bee lands on* MELISSA*'s shoulder.*

MELISSA: Clo.

CLO: Don't mind her, she's just saying hello.

> *She squats on one side of a hive box.*

One … two … three …

> *After they move the hive:*

You sure you're up to this?

MELISSA: I'm fine.

CLO: You just had a car crash.

MELISSA: So do it on your own.

Beat.

They start shifting hives onto a pallet.

When they have shifted four:

MELISSA: How many's that?
CLO: Four.
MELISSA: Out of?
CLO: A hundred and sixty.
MELISSA: This is bullshit.
CLO: Yep.
MELISSA: How long's that gonna take?
CLO: At this rate?
MELISSA: Ever heard of a forklift?
CLO: It's busted.
MELISSA: 'Course it is.
CLO: Here.

CLO offers her water.

MELISSA: How do I—?
CLO: Through the veil.
MELISSA: I feel like a dog shat in my head.
CLO: Teach you to drink so much.

MELISSA takes the bottle and sculls it down.

MELISSA: Daryl says you used to be a nurse.
CLO: Paramedic.
MELISSA: Cool.
CLO: I never finished studying.
MELISSA: Oh.
CLO: Where are you from?
MELISSA: Sydney.
CLO: Where?
MELISSA: Newtown.
CLO: Figures.
MELISSA: Fuck off.
CLO: I used to live there.
MELISSA: Newtown?
CLO: Darlinghurst.

MELISSA: Figures.
CLO: A terrace on Burton Street.
MELISSA: Near the art school?
CLO: Just behind it.
MELISSA: I used to go there.
CLO: Really?
MELISSA: Fuck, I miss good coffee.
CLO: I miss the bats. In the evenings. Flying low over the city. Wherever they want to go.

Beat.

MELISSA: I used to sneak into the gardens at sunset. Smoke a joint, lie on the grass and watch them glide overhead.
CLO: Why'd you leave?
MELISSA: My mum died.
CLO: Oh.
Right.

Beat.

MELISSA *swats another bee away.*

They like you.

MELISSA *stops.*

You okay?
MELISSA: I didn't think it would be like this.
Here. With the bees.
I thought it'd be more … I dunno.
Pastoral.

Beat.

CLO: Come with me.
MELISSA: Why? Where are we going?
CLO: I want to show you something.

SCENE SIX

Friday. Midday. The kitchen.
JOAN *is looking over the accounts.*

DARYL *enters. Waits. Beat.*

DARYL: Mum?

JOAN: I'm counting.

> *Long beat.*

Yes?

DARYL: It's nearly one.

JOAN: You want to go down and help?

> *Beat.*

Call her.

DARYL: She's not answering.

JOAN: She's working.

> *Beat.*

DARYL: She still singing to the bees?

JOAN: She says it calms them.

DARYL: She got them dancing yet?

> JOAN *almost smiles.*

Remember Dad? When they'd swarm and he'd whistle them down?

JOAN: Like he was conducting music.

DARYL: Millions of them. Swirling around him.

JOAN: And there he was at the centre …

DARYL: He was a magician.

> *Beat.*

JOAN: How's Karen?

DARYL: Carol. She's good. She says hi.

JOAN: Does she?

> JOAN *puts down her pen.*

DARYL: They the accounts? [*Reaching out*] Mind if I—?

> JOAN *slaps his hand away.*

Hey!

> JOAN *looks at him steadily.*

There's not enough bees.

JOAN: Can't be helped.
DARYL: The quote was six hundred.
JOAN: I know.
DARYL: Not four fifty.
JOAN: So we charge them less.
DARYL: That's not how it works.
JOAN: There's almost twenty-five million bees out there.
DARYL: Mum, we can't stuff this up. If they walk away—
JOAN: We've got a contract.
DARYL: For six hundred hives.
JOAN: They'll understand.
DARYL: And if they don't?
JOAN: …
DARYL: And what about next time?
JOAN: There's not gonna be a next time.
DARYL: Mum.
JOAN: That was the deal.
DARYL: I know.
JOAN: To help get us back on our feet.
DARYL: Let me help you.
JOAN: We do this once and then we're out.
DARYL: And go back to what?
JOAN: …
DARYL: Flogging honey to Crapalano?
JOAN: Shhh!
DARYL: The business is bust.
JOAN: We'll get through this.
DARYL: How?
JOAN: It's a rough patch.
DARYL: We're too small. Asian brands flooding the market and no wonder they're cheap, half of it's not even honey. How are we supposed to compete with that?
JOAN: Forty years we've been doing this.
DARYL: Mum, you said it yourself: Honey's a mug's game. And now we have this huge opportunity.
JOAN: I've got no more bees to spare.
DARYL: What about Clo's bees?

Beat.

JOAN: No.
DARYL: Why not?
JOAN: …
DARYL: You haven't told her, have you?
JOAN: After the sale.
DARYL: We need bees now. While there's still a margin. Before this thing gets here and wipes them out.
JOAN: It's a myth!

A few bees go rogue and the sky is falling! Now I've gone along with you because the Americans are morons and we can make a lot of money. But I refuse to believe—

No. I've been doing this for forty years. And never lost a single hive. And you know why? Because we don't get greedy and we don't take needless risks and so long as we look after the girls they look after us.

DARYL: And how's that working out?
JOAN: …
DARYL: How old are you?
JOAN: Don't patronise me.
DARYL: You never thought of retiring?
JOAN: I'll rest when I'm dead.
DARYL: I thought after Dad went—
JOAN: I'm still here.
DARYL: Why?
JOAN: …
DARYL: Clo.
JOAN: People remember the brand.
DARYL: They don't.
JOAN: It's important to her.
DARYL: It's a dead horse.
JOAN: You've been gone for years.
DARYL: And why was that?
JOAN: Here we go.
DARYL: Besides, I visited.
JOAN: Once. And left straight after the reading of the will.

DARYL: I was upset.
JOAN: You were furious.
DARYL: I'm trying to save us!
JOAN: You want to cash us in.
DARYL: They're disappearing, Mum.
JOAN: Bullshit.
DARYL: They can't take the stress.
JOAN: Bad beekeeping. That's all it is. The Yanks wouldn't know a sick bee if it stung them on the arse.
DARYL: And what about Europe? And Asia? It's everywhere.
JOAN: Not here.
DARYL: Not yet.
JOAN: Listen to that hum!

> KERRIE *enters, stops, unseen by both of them.*

DARYL: This thing, it hasn't reached here yet, but when it does … And then all of this … But. If we face this head-on. If we don't look away or hide our heads like everybody else, but instead we look straight down the barrel and see it for what it is … *an opportunity*. Then there's money to be made.
JOAN: You really believe that, don't you?
DARYL: We've got a window. But that's all.
JOAN: Come here.

> DARYL *kneels in front of her. She presses his head to her chest and runs her hand through his hair. She holds his face up to look at her.*

I know why you're doing this. And what you're trying to prove. And it's not that I'm not grateful. I am. But you'll never be Harry.
DARYL: What? Mum, I don't want to be.
JOAN: Shhh … You leave the business to me.
KERRIE: Ahem.

> DARYL, *startled, gets to his feet.*

JOAN: Yes?
KERRIE: Mick's on the phone.
JOAN: I'll call him back.
KERRIE: He wants to know when he can spray his crops.
JOAN: Monday.

KERRIE: He's pretty antsy. Says the beetles are out in force.
JOAN: Tomorrow. Once the truck has left.

> KERRIE *nods.* DARYL *is waiting.*

[*To* DARYL] Start on dinner.
DARYL: Yes, Mum.
JOAN: The girls will be hungry. They've been working all day.

> DARYL *exits.*

> JOAN *opens up the account book. She continues working.*

KERRIE: There's more hives sick.
JOAN: … How many?
KERRIE: Three.
JOAN: Fix it.

> KERRIE *turns to leave.*

How's Clo?
KERRIE: Exhausted.
JOAN: As soon as the sale goes through—
KERRIE: We're leaving.
JOAN: I'll talk to her.
KERRIE: We've made up our mind.
JOAN: One more year.
KERRIE: No.
JOAN: And the business is yours.
KERRIE: What about Daryl?
JOAN: What about him?
KERRIE: Can I go?
JOAN: Of course.

> But Clo stays here with me.

> *Beat.*

> KERRIE *exits.*

SCENE SEVEN

Cinque Terre.

A small shed surrounded by at least a hundred brightly coloured hive boxes. All of them are painted by hand.

CLO *leads* MELISSA *by the hand through the hives.*

CLO: And. Open.

    MELISSA *squeals in delight.*

You like?

MELISSA: They're so cute!

CLO: All handpainted.

MELISSA: They're like little condos for fairies.

CLO: Welcome to Cinque Terre.

MELISSA: *Grazi, bella.*

CLO: What?

MELISSA: … Are these to go on the truck?

CLO: Noooooooooo.

MELISSA: 'Uncle Harry's Honey'!

CLO: This is where it all began.

MELISSA: You're still making it?

CLO: Of course!

MELISSA: I thought you'd stopped.

CLO: Are you kidding?

MELISSA: It's so cool.

CLO: We run them all organic. No pesticides. No antibiotics. Just like Dad used to …

MELISSA: Cool guy.

CLO: Daz and I, when we were kids, we'd spend hours down here, listening to him talk while he worked. See, Mum ran the house, but the shed was Dad's. We'd hang on his every word …

MELISSA: I never knew my dad.

    CLO *approaches one of the hives, takes the lid off the top. Inside is a flurry of activity.*

CLO: Come here.

MELISSA: Won't they [sting?]

CLO: Trust me.

    MELISSA *approaches.*

Say hello to the girls.

    A warm buzz.

Beautiful, aren't they? A thousand bodies at work. Never complaining, never tiring. Listen to that hum.

Beat. They listen. Then ...

There. In the corner.

MELISSA: What is it?

CLO: [*singing*] 'A little ray of sunshine, has come into the world ...'

MELISSA: A baby bee!

CLO: Each of them lives about three weeks. She'll fly about eight hundred k and gather enough pollen to make one teaspoon of honey.

MELISSA: That's all?

CLO: That's a lifetime.

Beat.

MELISSA: What's with the record player?

CLO: You'll think it's dumb.

MELISSA: No way!

CLO: They like it.

MELISSA: What do you play them?

CLO: The Buzzcocks.

MELISSA: Serious?

CLO: Sting.

MELISSA: Ha!

CLO: [*with a laugh*] Anything. They just like the sound.

MELISSA: It's beautiful.

CLO: We're still hanging in there. Nothing like we used to. A few specialty shops. I'm building the brand up again slowly. The main thing is getting it back out there. Once people get the taste for it—
Here.

She scrapes the wax off a section of honeycomb and teases out a fat dollop of honey.

Try this.

MELISSA *does so.*

Bloodwood.

MELISSA: Mmm.

CLO: And also we've done yellowbox, stringybark, bluegum.

MELISSA: Mum always kept a jar in the cupboard.
CLO: Everybody did.
MELISSA: A teaspoon with her cuppa, but I always liked it best spread thick on toast.
CLO: Crumpets.
MELISSA: Yes! All dripping down your fingers.

> *A moment. They're getting along.*
>
> CLO *turns away, inspecting the frames.*

CLO: Do you want to talk about it? What happened with your mum.
MELISSA: Nah. It's cool.
CLO: I remember after Dad died. The bees were silent in their hives for days.
MELISSA: …
CLO: Anyway. We should get back to work. There's still a tonne of hives need loading up.
   Melissa?
   You okay?
MELISSA: MS.
CLO: … Oh.
MELISSA: That's how she … Sorry. Boring.
CLO: When?
MELISSA: Friday.
CLO: Last week?
MELISSA: I've been driving ever since.
CLO: You poor thing.
MELISSA: …
CLO: You're so young …
   But listen, the world is out there, waiting.
MELISSA: Why don't you leave?
CLO: What?
MELISSA: If you're not happy here.
CLO: I am … What makes you think I'm—?
MELISSA: Seriously?
CLO: This is my home.
MELISSA: …

> CLO *turns away, starts inspecting the hives.*

CLO: Okay, but I can't just leave.
MELISSA: Why not?
CLO: What about the business?
MELISSA: Your mum runs it.
CLO: But she still needs someone who's good with the bees.
MELISSA: It's not that hard.
CLO: Oh, now she's an expert.
MELISSA: I'm just saying / that if you want to go—
CLO: Plus there's Dad's honey. If I leave, who'll take care of that? Not to mention the girls?
MELISSA: I thought he was selling them. Daryl.
CLO: What? No. He's selling Mum's bees.
MELISSA: Okay.
CLO: These are mine.

Beat.

I'm gonna go. I am. After the sale. Once the business is back on its feet.
MELISSA: Clo?
CLO: There's just a few more things I have to—
MELISSA: Clover!
CLO: What?
MELISSA: The bees.
CLO: I told you they're just saying hello.
MELISSA: All of them?

CLO turns around. She gasps.

MELISSA stands perfectly still, in a cloud of gold. Bees.

She stands at the centre of a universe. A constellation of stars.

SCENE EIGHT

Friday night. The kitchen.

A celebration.

A bottle of champagne on ice. Music is playing on the stereo.

JOAN is sitting. DARYL and KERRIE are standing.

DARYL: And they're all loaded up?

KERRIE: Yep.
DARYL: Any problems?
KERRIE: Shitloads.
DARYL: But we're good?
JOAN: Knock wood.
DARYL: And we haven't lost any more?
KERRIE: Ask Clo.
DARYL: [*calling*] *Clo?!*
JOAN: She's in the shower.
DARYL: Oh, I nearly forgot!

He pulls out a bag of paper crown party hats.

One for you. And one for you. And one for— Whoah!

MELISSA *enters in a dress. One of* JOAN*'s.*

JOAN: Pick your jaw off the floor and offer the girl a seat.
DARYL: [*pulling a chair out*] Your throne.
JOAN: [*re: the dress*] Told you it'd fit.
DARYL: [*offering party crowns*] Green or gold?
JOAN: She can have mine.
DARYL: Let's get this party started!
KERRIE: Can we wait for Clo?

DARYL *pops the cork on the champagne.*

DARYL: Oops.
JOAN: Looks like you've been having a fine party on your own.
DARYL: Champagne?
JOAN: What's gotten into you?!
KERRIE: Six of my stubbies.
DARYL: I've been celebrating.

CLO *enters, sits. Clocks* MELISSA*'s dress.*

CLO: [*to* MELISSA] Nice dress.
JOAN: You didn't want it, remember?
DARYL: Is it weird she looks hot in it?
JOAN & MELISSA: [*together*] Yes!
CLO: [*to* KERRIE] How's your back?
KERRIE: Better.
JOAN: Sit down.

KERRIE: I'm fine.
DARYL: A family that sits together …
KERRIE: I can't.
DARYL: … What?
CLO: Kez?
KERRIE: … I …
DARYL: Oh, fuck.
KERRIE: It'll be better in the morning.
DARYL: You're joking. Tell me she's joking.
CLO: She can't drive, Mum.
DARYL: She has to.
JOAN: Are you up to it?
CLO: It's thirty-six hours!
KERRIE: I'll be fine.
DARYL: See?
CLO: Look at her.
KERRIE: I've got painkillers.
DARYL: We've got no other choice.
CLO: This is bullshit.
DARYL: No-one else can drive.
MELISSA: I can.

Beat.

JOAN: I beg your pardon.
CLO: You?
DARYL: Can drive a truck?
MELISSA: Not like a road train or anything …

DARYL *laughs.*

CLO: But the rig outside?
MELISSA: Eighteen-wheeler, yeah? Sure.
CLO: How?
MELISSA: I used to see this guy.
DARYL: I could kiss you.
JOAN: Leave the girl alone.
KERRIE: How long you had your licence?
MELISSA: I don't.
DARYL: Right.

CLO: And there it is.

Beat.

DARYL: Still …
CLO: You're not serious?
DARYL: If she spotted with Kez?
KERRIE: It could work.
DARYL: Taking turns behind the wheel.
CLO: She's not insured!
DARYL: That's the least of our worries.
CLO: And what if she rolls the truck?
DARYL: Mum?
JOAN: You sure you can handle it?

MELISSA *nods.*

Beat.

[*To* KERRIE] Rest up tonight. I want you on the road by three.
DARYL: And Melissa?
JOAN: Four-hour shifts.
CLO: You've all lost your minds.
JOAN: Don't crash my truck.
KERRIE: Hope you like Johnny Cash.
MELISSA: Johnny who?
KERRIE: The education begins.
DARYL: [*to* CLO] You tell Mum yet?
JOAN: What?
DARYL: We've got a very special guest.
CLO: He's drunk.
DARYL: Nope. Happy. That's allowed, isn't it?
JOAN: Well?
CLO: We were stacking hives and something happened.
JOAN: You had the suit on?
CLO: They didn't attack her.
JOAN: Then what?
CLO: I can't explain it.
DARYL: She's our new goodluck charm. I'll have to pin you to my chest.
JOAN: What happened?

MELISSA: Nothing.
   I panicked, that's all.
JOAN: Clove?
CLO: She fainted.
DARYL: You said she had them dancing—
JOAN: / The bees?
KERRIE: Let's have a toast.
DARYL: In a sec.
CLO: To Mum.
KERRIE: To Joan.
MELISSA: To Joan.
DARYL: … To Mum.
JOAN: To Harry.
DARYL: Saint Harry!

> JOAN *is about to start on him when* CLO *interjects.*

CLO: Did you want to say a few words?
JOAN: Why?
CLO: To celebrate.
JOAN: I'll celebrate when those bees are on the plane.
CLO: Mum …
JOAN: Fine … It's over forty years ago I met Harry. And together we built this business from a backyard in Perth to what it is today. And in that time we've weathered droughts, bushfires, and some brutal competition. And you know what? We're still here.
CLO: [*muttered*] Yay.
JOAN: I've asked a lot of you. I know. But here's the truth.

> DARYL'*s phone. It might ring or it may buzz.*
>
> DARYL *mouths: 'Sorry'.*

If we don't grow we die. / So here's to growing.

> DARYL *mimes: 'I have to take this'.*
>
> CLO *mouths: 'Now?'*

DARYL: [*raising his glass*] To growing.
JOAN: For as long as we can.

> DARYL *necks it. Leaves the glass on the table.*

OTHERS: Cheers.
DARYL: [*on the phone as he exits*] Speaking.

Beat.

The women sip their drinks.

Beat.

JOAN: You give Mick the okay?
KERRIE: He starts dusting tomorrow.
JOAN: And all the hives are secured? They've got a long road ahead.
CLO: We'll do it tonight.

Beat.

JOAN: I know how hard you work. And in a couple more years. Once I'm gone—
CLO: I don't want to talk about it.
JOAN: Why not?
CLO: It's morbid.
JOAN: I won't be here forever.

DARYL enters.

DARYL: More champagne?
JOAN: Who was that? On the phone.
DARYL: … Carol.
JOAN: Carol?
DARYL: You remember my wife?
CLO: Barely.
JOAN: And how is my lovely daughter-in-law?
DARYL: Good.
JOAN: That's it?
DARYL: She says hi.
JOAN: And my grandchildren?
DARYL: They're fine.
JOAN: You should have put them on.
DARYL: Next time.
JOAN: Call them.
DARYL: When are you gonna retire?
JOAN: I beg your pardon.
DARYL: You're sixty-five.

JOAN: A few more years.
KERRIE: Why not now?
CLO: Kerrie.
JOAN: There's still things I want to do.

Beat.

My goodness. Is this how you all feel? You're like vultures.
CLO: Mum.
JOAN: You can have it when I'm gone!
DARYL: There won't be anything left.
CLO: Daz, don't.
DARYL: Unless we keep exporting bees—
JOAN: Fuck the bees!

Beat.

DARYL: This deal. It's our only way out. If you knew how hard I fought, just to get us in the door and—
No, look at me! I bought us a future and you're throwing it away.
JOAN: I won't stab your father in the back.
DARYL: No, of course not. Better he do it himself and bleed out on the bedroom floor.
CLO: Jesus, Daryl.
JOAN: How dare you?
DARYL: ...
JOAN: No wonder your wife left you.
DARYL: What?
CLO: Mum.
JOAN: No. We have bit our tongues on this long enough. You couldn't even look after your own family. Why on earth would I trust you with mine?
DARYL: I don't know what you—
JOAN: You're a cheat! And a liar as well.
DARYL: Clo, what's she on about?
CLO: Stop it, Daryl.

Beat.

DARYL: ... You knew?
JOAN: Of course we fucking—

DARYL: Carol told you.
CLO: She was worried about you.
DARYL: I'll bet.
JOAN: Pathetic. As soon as it gets a bit hard people bolt for the door.

> MELISSA *gets up too.*

MELISSA: I should—
JOAN & DARYL: [*together*] STAY!

> MELISSA *sits.*

JOAN: It's a marriage, not a hayride. You have to tough it out!
DARYL: Like you and Dad?
CLO: Stop it.
JOAN: Your father was a good man.
DARYL: He just liked to fuck around.
JOAN: He was confused.
DARYL: Is that why he killed himself? Bit down on the muzzle of a shotgun and—
CLO: *Stop!*
DARYL: He spent his whole life trying to escape you.
CLO: Leave her alone.
DARYL: You're sticking up for her? Baba Yaga? How much Kool Aid did you drink?
CLO: Sorry about Carol. This new guy. I'm sure it won't last.

> DARYL *rises.*

DARYL: Fuck you.
KERRIE: Back off.
DARYL: I feel sorry for you. As soon as this sale goes through, at least I'm out of here, but you, you're gonna rot here forever.

> *Beat.*

CLO: You're still short.
DARYL: What?
CLO: A hundred and forty hives, right?
Told Hank the Yank yet?
DARYL: I brought you this deal!
CLO: Fuck the deal.

DARYL: And what are you gonna live on?
CLO: Dad's honey—
DARYL: What honey?
JOAN: Daryl, don't.
DARYL: No, I'm sorry but it's time she knew.
CLO: Knew what?
DARYL: The brand is dead.
CLO: Then why are people still buying it?
DARYL: They're not.

Beat.

CLO: [*with a laugh*] What?
DARYL: We sold the last jar three months back.
JOAN: You selfish little shit.
DARYL: You should have told her.
CLO: Mum?
JOAN: It's a temporary setback.
DARYL: When you called me—*desperate* for help. Weeping on the phone.
JOAN: We'll bounce back.
DARYL: No-one's buying it. No-one.
CLO: You said we were expanding.
DARYL: Oh, come on, Clo. No-one's that dumb.
CLO: But the truck? Mum?
DARYL: Tell her.
JOAN: The truck takes it to Capilano.
CLO: No.
DARYL: And they mix it in with everything else.

Long beat.

CLO *runs out of the room.*

KERRIE *approaches* DARYL. *He may or may not flinch.*

KERRIE: You're a cunt.

She exits after CLO.

Beat.

JOAN *and* MELISSA *sit sipping champagne.*

The longest beat in the world.

SCENE NINE

Friday night. Late. Cinque Terre.

CLO *is alone amongst the hives. She holds a jar of 'Uncle Harry's Honey'.*

KERRIE *enters.*

CLO *looks up.*

She stirs a honey dipper, removes it and watches the honey drip back into the jar.

Long beat.

CLO: Did you know?

>KERRIE *approaches.*

I feel like such a fool.

KERRIE: …
CLO: It's been months.
KERRIE: She knew you'd leave.
CLO: I don't know why you stay.

>KERRIE *leaves* CLO*'s side.*

Where are you going?

>KERRIE *switches on the record player—old jazz.*

KERRIE: Come here.
CLO: Your back.
KERRIE: I feel light as a feather.

>CLO *stands, approaches* KERRIE. *She folds into her arms. They hold each other close. They sway to the music.*

CLO: Why are you so happy?
KERRIE: Are you kidding?
>You can go now.
>All that weight.
>It's not yours.

CLO: Tell me about the house.
KERRIE: It's a terrace in the city.
CLO: Where?
KERRIE: Surry Hills.

CLO: Mmm.
KERRIE: And it's small. But cosy. Polished wood floors. Downstairs there's a fireplace in the living room. And a piano for you to practise on.
CLO: What'll you do?
KERRIE: I'll listen to you.
CLO: …
KERRIE: And there are paintings everywhere. And books.
CLO: You don't read.
KERRIE: And in the kitchen there's a gas oven.
CLO: Finally!
KERRIE: [*nodding*] And we'll grow our own vegies.
CLO: Stuff that! We'll buy them from Coles.
KERRIE: And we'll have a huge dining table.
CLO: No.
KERRIE: No?
CLO: A small one. Just for us.
KERRIE: And the bathroom's hot pink!
CLO: You dill.
KERRIE: And there's an old iron tub right in the centre of the room, big enough for two.
CLO: … And the bedroom?
KERRIE: White. With one of those mosquito nets hanging over the bed.
CLO: And a fan.
KERRIE: And a tin roof.
CLO: And big bay windows we can open in the summer and watch the lightning over the city.
KERRIE: And listen to the rain pouring down …

    Beat.

So … should I be worried? You and the bee whisperer.
CLO: She's twelve. Besides, you're the one driving with her.
KERRIE: But I'm dancing with you.

    Beat. A smile.

    They dance in silence until the song ends. KERRIE *untangles herself.*

CLO: Don't go.

KERRIE: Long drive tomorrow.
CLO: …
KERRIE: The sooner I'm back here the sooner we can kiss this place goodbye.
CLO: Stay.
KERRIE: We've still gotta seal the hives. Check the truck.
CLO: In the morning. Please?
KERRIE: [*relenting*] One more dance.

> *They might kiss.*
>
> *They might dance together during the following scene.*

SCENE TEN

Friday night. The kitchen. Late.

MELISSA *and* DARYL *are alone.* JOAN *has gone to bed. They are both a little drunk. He is holding her hand in his.*

MELISSA: I think it's infected.
DARYL: It's not infected.
MELISSA: Well, she must have left the stinger in or—
DARYL: There's nothing there.
MELISSA: It kills!
DARYL: The first one's the worst.
MELISSA: She's not doing it again!
DARYL: A couple more—
MELISSA: No fucken way!
DARYL: Until she knows you're not allergic.
MELISSA: She said I wasn't!
DARYL: It takes a few to be sure.
MELISSA: Bitch.
DARYL: She's a character.
MELISSA: So's Voldemort.
DARYL: Hm.
MELISSA: What if I *am* allergic?
DARYL: Then you're useless to her.
MELISSA: Like you?

> *Beat.*

DARYL: Look, it can't hurt that much. She does it to herself. It helps with her rheumatism.
MELISSA: Batshit crazy.
DARYL: She's got epipens in the bureau. If you'd reacted at all she'd have stuck you right away.
MELISSA: Is that what happened to you?
DARYL: No.

Beat.

MELISSA: It's okay. You don't have to—
DARYL: Happened when I was a kid.

See Clo, she cares for the bees now, but back then it was me. I was Dad's right-hand man.
MELISSA: Harry and son.
DARYL: I used to think he was a wizard ... He'd only have to whistle and they'd start swirling around him. Like the centre of a universe. And the bees all hanging like stars. This bright, glittering sphere.

But whenever I tried, they'd just ignore me. Dad thought it was hilarious! I used to beg him to teach me. I knew there must be a trick.

There was this girl.
MELISSA: From school.
DARYL: No, she worked on the farm. I suppose I wanted to impress her.
MELISSA: Cute.
DARYL: One arvo I got home from school early. Saw Dad duck out behind the hives. I thought to practise his trick ... He had someone with him. I thought maybe he was telling them his secret, and then he's pushed up against her and ... I thought he'd tripped. You believe that? That she'd help him up and he'd apologise ... He was fucking her. Bare ass stabbing away at her. And then he's pulled her hair back and ... [it was her]

I musta cried out. And they've pulled apart and ... he just looks at me ... I bolted. Right into the hives.
MELISSA: Oh, fuck.
DARYL: Took out a whole tower. I remember they hung there in the air ... and then *bam!*

It sounded like a chainsaw. This roar coming out of the hives. I tried to wave them away but they just kept coming.

My arm, my neck, I must have screamed. That's how one got in my mouth. I tried to run but ... Sorry.

MELISSA: It's okay.

DARYL: Dad saved me! Even after all that he still gets to be the hero.

MELISSA: How?

DARYL: Threw me in the dam.

MELISSA: Ha!

DARYL: [*with a laugh*] You believe it? They reckon it saved my life. I woke up on the plane, with Mum holding my hand. I couldn't see—
My eyes ... It's the only time I've ever known her to cry.
Anyway ...
It was touch and go for couple of days and then when it looked like I'd pull through Mum caught a Greyhound back home.

MELISSA: Without you?

DARYL: It was the middle of the season.

MELISSA: ...

DARYL: I spent a week in hospital then they shipped me off to boarding school ... Doctors reckoned I had so much venom in me, my immune system shat itself. Went into overdrive. See, it's not the sting that kills you. It's this. Your own blood turned against you.

Beat.

MELISSA: You were their son.

DARYL: ... Good thing they had a daughter too.

Beat.

Family, eh?

MELISSA: Well, I'd say you burned that bridge.

DARYL: You reckon?

MELISSA: Whoosh!

DARYL: Fuck 'em.

Beat.

MELISSA: It still hurts.

DARYL: What?

MELISSA: My wrist.

DARYL: Poor little princess.

MELISSA: Get stuffed.

DARYL: Put this on it.
MELISSA: What is it?
DARYL: Honey.
MELISSA: Really, Stingose is fine.
DARYL: It's an antibiotic.
MELISSA: No thanks.
DARYL: Here.

> DARYL *reaches out for her.* MELISSA *pulls away. He snatches at her, misses. He lunges again, she struggles. He tries to kiss her. She punches him.*

MELISSA: Whoah!
DARYL: What the fuck?!
MELISSA: You tried to kiss me.
DARYL: You punched me!
MELISSA: I told ya to stay back.
DARYL: No, you didn't!
MELISSA: Yeah, I did. With my eyes.
DARYL: It's okay.
MELISSA: No, it's not.
DARYL: I'm sorry.
MELISSA: Aren't you married?
DARYL: Separated.
MELISSA: And *old*!
DARYL: I thought—
MELISSA: What, that I'd just feel sorry for you and—?
DARYL: No! Oh, I dunno, maybe.
MELISSA: Gross!
DARYL: I'm sorry!
    Don't go? Stay?

> *Beat.*

MELISSA: Who was she? With your dad?
DARYL: It's funny. Mum and Clo make him out to be a saint but, Jesus, the fights.
MELISSA: What about?
DARYL: The business. Money. Girls.
MELISSA: Girls?

DARYL: They don't tell you that on the label.
MELISSA: How many?
DARYL: Never enough.

> *Beat.*

MELISSA: Why'd she let him get away with it? Your mum?
DARYL: She loved him.

> *Beat.*

MELISSA: I should … [go to bed].
DARYL: Sure. Long drive tomorrow.

> MELISSA *touches his face.*

What was that for?
MELISSA: You're sweet.
DARYL: …
MELISSA: One day they'll see.

SCENE ELEVEN

Saturday. Early morning. The darkness before dawn.

Outside, sounds of a truck door opening and slamming shut, keys turned in the ignition. The engine fails to turn over. Another attempt.

Another.

Beat.

Another.

Beat.

Another.

SCENE TWELVE

Saturday morning. Home.
Everyone.

CLO: It's not her fault!
DARYL: When's the last time you had it serviced?
KERRIE: It drove fine on Thursday.
JOAN: How long?

KERRIE: At least a day.
DARYL: We don't have a day!
KERRIE: I'll have to dismantle it and clean every part.
MELISSA: I can help.
DARYL: If you'd left last night like you were supposed to.
CLO: What is it? Dirt?
KERRIE: Wax.
JOAN: Wax?
KERRIE: The whole engine's gummed up.
CLO: Wasps?
KERRIE: If you don't need me, I'll—
JOAN: Go.

>   KERRIE *exits.*
>
>   *Beat.*

DARYL: So we hire another truck.
CLO: There's no time.
DARYL: Well, borrow one. From the Mathesons or—
CLO: They sold up years ago.
DARYL: The Pikes—
CLO: Don't you get it? Everyone's left.
DARYL: Come on, think! We're gonna miss the flight!
MELISSA: I reckon that horse has bolted.
DARYL: Not if we leave now!
CLO: In *what*?!
JOAN: I'll call QANTAS.
DARYL: Fuck!
JOAN: See if they can put us on a later flight.
DARYL: When?
JOAN: Monday.
DARYL: That's two days away.
JOAN: It'll work.
DARYL: And what do I tell Hank?
CLO: Tell him we hit a roo.
DARYL: You think this is funny? There's five hundred hives out there!
CLO: Four fifty.
JOAN: We can do this.

CLO: They're already stressed.
JOAN: There's still late wattle flowering in the hills. They'll have to range a little further, that's all …
CLO: I don't know.
JOAN: Forty-eight hours. So long as nothing else happens, we'll be fine.

A drone in the distance.

DARYL: I could drive up to Nannup.
CLO: And then what?
DARYL: Flag down a truck.
MELISSA: Listen.
DARYL: On the highway. There's trucks pass through all the time.

CLO *laughs.*

You've hated this sale from the start.
CLO: You've been gone twenty-five years.
JOAN: Shhh.
DARYL: It's not my fault I'm allergic.
CLO: Well, it's not fucken mine!
DARYL: Who are you to say that / to me?
CLO: I'm who stayed when you—
JOAN: *Quiet!*

Beat.

DARYL: What?

They listen.

MELISSA: Is that a plane?
JOAN: Crop duster.
DARYL: / Oh, shit!
CLO: Mick!

SCENE THIRTEEN

Saturday. Early morning. The trailer.

A steady buzz.

CLO *and* MELISSA *are taping the hives. Both wear hats and veils.* MELISSA *stops to catch her breath.*

CLO: We're not done.
MELISSA: It feels like we're sealing their tombs.
CLO: The longer they stay open the more poison gets brought back into the hive.
MELISSA: Poison?
CLO: Pesticide.
MELISSA: So we starve them instead.
CLO: I'll supp them with sugar.
MELISSA: You said sugar was bad for—
CLO: I'm trying to save lives!
MELISSA: O-o-okay.

Back to work.

Beat.

Won't they just put in another order?
CLO: Who?
MELISSA: America.
CLO: …
MELISSA: Clo?
CLO: After this, we're done.
MELISSA: But won't they—?
CLO: Did you hear? This is a one-off. We get these sold and then I'm out.

They go back to work.

Beat.

MELISSA: I'm sorry. About your dad's honey …
CLO: …
MELISSA: I thought it was yum.
CLO: …

Beat.

MELISSA: How long have you and Kerrie—?
CLO: That's none of your business.
MELISSA: Sorry.
CLO: What time'd *you* get to bed last night?
    You and Daz?
MELISSA: Oh. We didn't— Nothing happened. Like. At all.
CLO: Forget it.

MELISSA: Trust me. That'd be a disaster.
CLO: The sooner we get these done the sooner you can go.

> *Long beat.*
>
> *They continue taping the hives.*
>
> JOAN *enters.*

Mum?
JOAN: A word.

> CLO *hands the tape to* MELISSA.

Not you. Her.
CLO: Eat your heart out.

> CLO *exits for the house.*
>
> MELISSA *waits.*
>
> JOAN *starts inspecting the hives. She's looking for something.*
>
> *Beat.*

JOAN: How are they?
MELISSA: Nervous.
JOAN: The queens are still laying brood?

> MELISSA *nods.*
>
> JOAN *pulls out a frame, inspecting it.*

You don't have much of a plan, do you?
MELISSA: It's how I roll.
JOAN: Drop the act, you're dealing with me, not my cunt-addled son.
MELISSA: …
JOAN: How'd you like to stay?
MELISSA: Here?
JOAN: Sure.
MELISSA: Are you kidding?
JOAN: It might be fun.
MELISSA: That's one word for it.
JOAN: You've got a knack.

> *Beat.*

MELISSA: What about Clover? And Daryl?

JOAN: I expect she'll be glad of the help.
MELISSA: If she stays?
JOAN: She'll stay.
MELISSA: She might surprise you.
JOAN: You leave the children to me.

> *Beat.*

> JOAN *picks up a frame. The bees buzz angrily for a moment.*

MELISSA: You should be careful.
JOAN: They won't sting me.

> *She puts the frame back. Pulls out another. Continues her inspection.*

You should have seen them with Harry. He could get them to do anything he wanted. Anything at all.

…

When I met him, I would have been your age. He wasn't even Harry then, he was still Aristaeus, selling honey door-to-door.
MELISSA: I don't care how you met.
JOAN: Oh, I reckon you do.
MELISSA: …
JOAN: Of course I couldn't understand a word he said, both of us were fresh off the boat, but even then he had this power.

You've got it too.
MELISSA: …
JOAN: How'd you find us?
MELISSA: What?
JOAN: …
MELISSA: What are you talking about? … I don't know what you mean?
JOAN: Finished?

> *Beat.*

MELISSA: The cheques.

> *Beat.*

JOAN: Why'd you wait so long?
MELISSA: I only just found out. Going through Mum's things …
JOAN: She dead?

MELISSA: Last week.
JOAN: Good.
MELISSA: Fuck off.
JOAN: I always knew you'd come.
MELISSA: …
JOAN: Well?
MELISSA: What?
JOAN: You must have questions.

>   MELISSA *nods*.

He loved you.
MELISSA: … Yeah right.
JOAN: And your mother. It broke his heart giving you up. I don't think he ever forgave me.
MELISSA: …
JOAN: Perhaps that's why he did what he did.

>   *Beat.*

MELISSA: Did he leave a note?
JOAN: No.
MELISSA: Oh.
JOAN: But you have the letters.
MELISSA: You knew?
JOAN: Oh, the fights we had over those. The cheques I could understand, but the effort he put into those letters. Late at night, hunched over the kitchen table, scrawling out another epistle to his little girl.
MELISSA: …
JOAN: Your father loved you. And having to give you up, I think he regretted it for the rest of his life.
MELISSA: …
JOAN: Which is why I'm asking you to stay.
MELISSA: …
JOAN: Your dad started something here. But I can't do this on my own anymore. I'm old. And it's too fucking hard.
So what do you say?
Help me keep your father's dream alive.

>   *Beat.*

MELISSA: I'll think about it.
JOAN: Good. That's all I ask.

SCENE FOURTEEN

The house.

DARYL *is at the table, with a tin of varnish.* CLO *enters. Sits opposite him.*

DARYL: Are they—?
CLO: Done.
DARYL: Thank you.
CLO: It's a band-aid solution.
DARYL: I know.
CLO: A few hours. Any more and they'll suffocate.

   Beat.

   DARYL *slides the tin across to her.*

What is it?
DARYL: Protect-A-Coat.
CLO: Okay.
DARYL: I thought you could use it on your hives.
   It stops the colour fading.
CLO: Is that a joke?
DARYL: No.
CLO: You should have told me.
DARYL: Probably.
CLO: What happened to your eye?
DARYL: Nothing.
CLO: Did Mum—?
DARYL: No.
   It was Melissa.
CLO: Ha!
DARYL: She's tougher than she looks.
CLO: Same old Daz.
DARYL: What does that mean?
CLO: Nothing.
DARYL: I'm nothing like Dad.
CLO: That's not what I meant.

Beat.

Why do you hate him so much?
CLO: ...
CLO: Tell me. Did he ... touch you?
DARYL: What? No!
CLO: Then what?
DARYL: Why didn't you visit?
CLO: ... I did.
DARYL: But not since the kids.
CLO: You could have come here.
DARYL: They want to meet you.
CLO: Me too.
DARYL: But Mum.
CLO: You know how hard it is to get away.
DARYL: It nearly killed me!

CLO *smiles.*

What'll you do now?
CLO: What?
... I'm waiting for Kerrie with the truck.
DARYL: And after that?
CLO: ... I don't know.

Beat.

DARYL: How's her back?
CLO: Better.
DARYL: I guess you're only as old as the woman you feel.
CLO: Fuck off.
Sorry about Carol.
DARYL: ... Thanks.
CLO: I never liked her anyway.
DARYL: You made that pretty clear.
CLO: Plus the whole Carol/Daryl thing.
DARYL: It'd never have worked.

CLO *stands. About to exit.*

[*Re: the varnish*] Forgetting something?
CLO: No thanks.

DARYL: But I got it for the hives.
CLO: It'll kill 'em.
DARYL: Oh. Fuck. Sorry.
CLO: You trying to tell me something?
DARYL: What's the point? You don't listen.
CLO: [*exiting*] What was that?
DARYL: I said—
  Oh.

> DARYL *smiles.*

SCENE FIFTEEN

Midday.

KERRIE *is out amongst the hives.* MELISSA *enters.*

MELISSA: How's the engine?
KERRIE: Parts are soaking now.
MELISSA: How long?
KERRIE: Couple more hours.
MELISSA: I'll tell Joan.

> MELISSA *turns to go.*

KERRIE: You two looked thick as thieves.
MELISSA: She's smart.
KERRIE: She needs her head examined.
  What they're doing in the States, it ain't natural. Fields that go on forever. And the only way to maintain it is by freighting in more bees.
MELISSA: What'll happen to them?
KERRIE: Sunflowers in Oregon, pumpkins in Texas—just shift her from crop to crop, year round. But you can't industrialise Nature. Not on that level. Sooner or later she'll rebel.
MELISSA: Is that why they're disappearing?
KERRIE: Would you hang around?
MELISSA: Why do you?
KERRIE: … How'd you go with the hives?
MELISSA: They're not happy.
KERRIE: I'd be furious.
MELISSA: They're trying to get out but they're trapped.

KERRIE: …
MELISSA: I saw a few trying to get back inside.
KERRIE: They won't survive on their own.
MELISSA: What about bees in the wild?
KERRIE: These are battery hens.

> *Beat.*
>
> You know how this thing started?
>
> In Korea. There's this tiny little mite. Size of a poppy seed.
>
> Asian honey bees—they're more aggro than ours, they don't put up with any shit. Only we prefer Europeans. They're easier to handle, make more honey. 'Course she wasn't always that way, but we've bred the wildness out of her, reduced her to a cow we come to milk.
>
> Now she sits politely while we steal her honey. Sits politely while her sisters die one by one, while her hive is overrun.
>
> We don't learn. We just keep doing what we're doing, hoping magic will save us. But it won't.
>
> *Beat.*

MELISSA: What was he like? Harry.
KERRIE: I met him right near the end … He'd potter around in his shed and check in to see how we were going, but mostly he was in his own world. All this charm they go on about, I didn't see that. He was just this lonely old man …
MELISSA: Did he know? About you and Clo?
KERRIE: One night he baled me up behind the stacks. I thought he was gonna take a swing at me. Instead he begged me to get her out of here.
MELISSA: Why didn't you?
KERRIE: I did.
MELISSA: Sydney.
KERRIE: Joan wasn't happy, but with Harry's blessing, there wasn't much she could do. I got us a place in the city. Clo was studying. I had a job landscaping. And we were there. And it was real.

> …
>
> Then Harry died.

MELISSA: Fuck.
KERRIE: What are you doing here?
MELISSA: Joan sent me.

KERRIE: You know what I mean.
MELISSA: I was headed to—
KERRIE: Perth. I know. To do what? Exactly? Swim with the dolphins?
MELISSA: No.
KERRIE: You drove all this way for—
MELISSA: The sunset.
KERRIE: The sunset. Right? You know they've got those in Sydney?
MELISSA: Not over the water.
KERRIE: You coulda stopped in Adelaide.
MELISSA: No. My mum, she always said it was beautiful. I just wanted to see it once, before I …
KERRIE: Before you what?
MELISSA: … I don't know.

Beat.

KERRIE: What'd Joan want?
MELISSA: She wants me to stay.
KERRIE: You want my advice, you'll hop in the truck with me tonight and never look back. This place is *sticky*, the longer you stay here, the harder it gets to leave.
MELISSA: Because of Clo.
KERRIE: …
MELISSA: Kerrie?

MELISSA *laughs.*

KERRIE: You come in here, waving that pert little arse around, bouncing those perfect tits right under her nose.
MELISSA: [*with a laugh*] You are way off!
KERRIE: I'm onto you.
MELISSA: She'll never leave, you know.
KERRIE: She will.
MELISSA: Joan won't let her.
KERRIE: As soon as the sale goes through—
MELISSA: Then it'll be something else.
KERRIE: …
MELISSA: She's gonna die here.
And if you wait, so will you?

> CLO *enters. Stops.*

CLO: Kez? Mum needs you.
KERRIE: What is it?
CLO: More bees.

> CLO *exits. They follow after her.*

SCENE SIXTEEN

Home. JOAN, CLO *and* DARYL.

The buzzing is more intense. The bees sound angry.

DARYL: I didn't know, alright?
JOAN: You're a fool.
DARYL: They told me they were fine.
CLO: Who?
DARYL: They were supposed to be healthy. That's what they said!
JOAN: Where did you get them?
DARYL: Gumtree.
JOAN: You're joking?
DARYL: Mum—
CLO: Fucking Gumtree?!
JOAN: I've got almost five hundred hives out there!
CLO: Wasn't that enough?
DARYL: No.
CLO: You stupid greedy fuck.
DARYL: If you'd have given me yours.
CLO: So this is my fault?
DARYL: How else was I gonna make up the numbers?
CLO: Not like this!
DARYL: The order was six hundred.
JOAN: You've put everything at risk!
DARYL: We're already at risk!
CLO: Gumtree?
DARYL: We're short a hundred and forty hives!
And that's before we lose another eight per cent on the plane. Understand? We are way under target.
CLO: Hey, why don't you check eBay?

DARYL: I had no choice!
CLO: You call them up and explain.
DARYL: Explain what? That we couldn't even fill the minimum order? That we're so incompetent—
CLO: Who cares? It's done!
DARYL: *We'll lose the contract!*

    Beat.

CLO: What contract?

    Beat.

Mum?
DARYL: Come on, guys …
JOAN: No.
DARYL: Who do you think paid for all this? All the new breeding stock, all those hundreds of hive boxes. Not to mention the supplements. Did you think that came for free?
CLO: You said it was an investment.
DARYL: It was.
CLO: In the future.
DARYL: Not ours. It was a loan. And they expect a return.
CLO: No.
DARYL: You think one sale is gonna fix everything? By the time we pay air freight and tax and insurance and buy new stock we'll be lucky to come out with anything …

And how long till we build up the next population? Till the hives are queen-right and the frames are full?
CLO: You said this deal would save us.
DARYL: It will.
CLO: You promised.
DARYL: In the long term.
CLO: No.
DARYL: That's when we make the money. Not this time but next time. And the time after that.
JOAN: You'd already signed it. Hadn't you? Before you even brought it to me.
CLO: They're just money to you, aren't they?
DARYL: This is a business.

JOAN: How much do we owe?
DARYL: We'll pay it back as soon as these are sold.
CLO: They're sick, Daz.
DARYL: I didn't know that!
JOAN: What happens? If we renege?
DARYL: … It won't come to that.
JOAN: What happens?
DARYL: [*to* CLO] If you had have just given us *your* bees—
CLO: Dad's bees!
DARYL: I did what had to be done!

    KERRIE *and* MELISSA *enter.*

JOAN: Well?
KERRIE: Chalkbrood.
CLO: How bad?
KERRIE: They're riddled with it.
DARYL: So? We spray them with fungicide or—
CLO: We have to destroy them.
DARYL: What?! No!
KERRIE: The risk of infection—
DARYL: So give them medicine or—
CLO: If I lose *one* of Dad's bees …
DARYL: We'll be fine. Trust me.

    JOAN *swats her neck.*

MELISSA: Joan?
CLO: You alright?

    JOAN *looks down at the dying bee in her hand.*

DARYL: Mum?
JOAN: Get rid of them.
DARYL: What? No! Wait, let's just—
    What do I do with them?
JOAN: I don't care.
DARYL: Just dump them by the side of the road?
JOAN: I want them gone. Now.
DARYL: But—
JOAN: [*to* CLO] Dose all our bees with antibiotics.
CLO: Yes, Mum.

JOAN: Take Melissa as well.
DARYL: What about me?
JOAN: I want you gone by morning.
DARYL: … What?
JOAN: You can stay the night, then tomorrow you'll go.
DARYL: I brought you the deal!
JOAN: And I won't let you jeopardise it anymore.
DARYL: You can't do that.
CLO: Mum?
JOAN: You brought this on yourself.
DARYL: Mum, please?
JOAN: You invited disaster into our house.
DARYL: But I did it for us.
   Mum?
   Clo? You alright with this?
CLO: …
DARYL: I'll fight it.
JOAN: No, you won't.
DARYL: Dad left it to me and—
JOAN: You?! I look at you and I'm ashamed.

Beat.

DARYL *storms out.*

The four women, alone.

Well?

Beat.

Back to work.

JOAN *heads outside to the hives.*

MELISSA *follows.*

CLO *and* KERRIE, *alone.*

SCENE SEVENTEEN

Saturday night. Late.
The hum of bees in their hives. Muted. Dulled.

The bees are agitated—their buzzing grows louder and louder as they rage inside their prison, chewing at the tape that holds them, desperate to be free.

And then they're through.

Exodus.

Like a cork released.

The bees escape into the night.

SCENE EIGHTEEN

Sunday. Early morning. The kitchen.

Silence. The background hum of bees at work is gone. A silence that will last until the end of the play.

JOAN *looks visibly ill. The others haven't yet noticed.*

KERRIE: Gone.
DARYL: How did they—?
KERRIE: Chewed their way out.
MELISSA: All of them?
KERRIE: The queens are still in the hive.
CLO: Oh, God.
DARYL: That's good, isn't it?
CLO: No, Daryl.
DARYL: It means they'll come back.
KERRIE: It means the colony's deserted them.
JOAN: Impossible.
KERRIE: If you don't believe me—
JOAN: I don't.
KERRIE: Go look for yourself.
JOAN: They don't abandon the queen.
KERRIE: They left the honey as well.
MELISSA: Poison?
CLO: That many bees? The grass would crunch underfoot.
KERRIE: You know what this is.
JOAN: Take the ute and see if you can find them.
CLO: How?!
JOAN: Check the forest.

CLO: And then what?
JOAN: First you find them, then we'll deal with that.
CLO: Mum—
JOAN: They won't survive!
KERRIE: We need to report it.
JOAN: No.
KERRIE: If it's what it looks like …
JOAN: It's not.
CLO: Mum, you know what this is—
JOAN: Chalkbrood.
CLO: They're not dead. They're gone.
JOAN: We don't know what it is.
KERRIE: I'd say it's pretty damn clear.
CLO: Mum. There are protocols.
KERRIE: The whole colony's collapsed.
JOAN: I don't want to hear it!

Beat.

We don't have time for this.

She stumbles.

DARYL: Mum?
JOAN: I'm fine.
CLO: Are you / sure?
JOAN: *Now!*
CLO: [*to* KERRIE] Check the hives for mites.
JOAN: You won't find any.
CLO: Melissa and I will take the ute.

They start off.

JOAN: Not her.
CLO: Mum?
JOAN: The girl stays with me.
MELISSA: Okay.
CLO: Why?
JOAN: That's between me and her.
CLO: What are you up to?
DARYL: Mum, you don't look so good.

JOAN: I'm fine.
DARYL: Maybe you should sit down?
JOAN: Go with your sister.
CLO: Who is she?
JOAN: No-one.
KERRIE: Then why'd you ask her to stay?
JOAN: She can help.
CLO: Who are you?
JOAN: She's going to bring the bees / back.

> JOAN *starts to swoon.*

DARYL: Grab her!

> *The others rush to catch her.*

SCENE NINETEEN

Joan's bedroom. Late.

JOAN *is asleep, wheezing faintly.* CLO *is sitting by her side.*

CLO: Look at you. Even in your sleep you're frowning. Are we really that disappointing?

> MELISSA *enters, watches.*

MELISSA: How is she?
CLO: Her breathing's better.
MELISSA: I thought she wasn't allergic?
CLO: I guess even Mum can only hold so much venom.
MELISSA: You look tired.
CLO: I'm always tired.
MELISSA: …
CLO: You find them?
MELISSA: No.
CLO: And if you had?
MELISSA: …
CLO: You gonna whistle them down like Dad?
MELISSA: … I wanted to tell you.
CLO: She's grooming you, isn't she?
MELISSA: I think so.

CLO: I always wanted a sister.
MELISSA: Get some sleep. I'll watch her till morning.
CLO: I'm not going anywhere.
MELISSA: That's up to you.

> *Beat.*
>
> CLO *stands up, to hit her or what? She exits, leaving* MELISSA *alone with* JOAN.
>
> *Beat.*
>
> MELISSA *approaches the bed.*
>
> *Beat.*
>
> *She sits by the bed.*

JOAN: [*eyes still closed*] She gone?
MELISSA: You're awake?
JOAN: Stay.
MELISSA: I'll get Clo.
JOAN: I can't face that yet.
MELISSA: She's worried.
JOAN: You don't like me much, do you?
MELISSA: I hardly know you.
JOAN: Reckon if I were you I wouldn't like me much either.
MELISSA: I think you're a bitch.
JOAN: Help me up.

> MELISSA *hesitates, then helps her sit up in bed.*

You blame me, I get that. For keeping your mum and dad apart. I did what had to be done. For the good of the family. That's what a mother does.

See, you may not like me but you and I—we're both peas in a pod. You're strong. Probably from dragging that dead weight since the day you were born. Oh yeah, I remember her. Harry always had a thing for little broken birds.

MELISSA: Fuck you.
JOAN: I never got it. What he saw in her. Maybe I'm biased. But he loved her, through and through.
MELISSA: Then why'd he never come out and see us?

JOAN: Maybe if you'd answered his letters …
MELISSA: I never got them.
JOAN: … Well, I'm sure she had her reasons.
MELISSA: He still could have called.
JOAN: You were his princess.

But princesses live in castles far away. Besides, then you'd meet him and learn what a fuck-up he was and Harry couldn't have that.

I see him in Daryl. Clo too. Every time I look at them, that weakness. But I don't see it in you.

MELISSA: What are you saying?
JOAN: I love my children. But Clo's too soft and Daz is a dropkick. And you're still Harry's girl.

Beat.

So are you with me or not?

Beat.

MELISSA Can you walk?
JOAN: Good girl.
MELISSA: Get your boots on.
JOAN: If your father could see you now.
MELISSA: Hurry. We don't have much time.
JOAN: Where are we going?
MELISSA: Cinque Terre.

Before they burn it to the ground.

SCENE TWENTY

Cinque Terre.

KERRIE *is stacking hive boxes, building a pyre.*

CLO *enters, watching.*

Eventually …

CLO: How much longer?
KERRIE: These are the last ones.
CLO: And then?
KERRIE: We burn the lot.
CLO: …

KERRIE: Clo, this is big ... If we don't quarantine now—
CLO: This is everything we built.

>KERRIE *whacks one of the hive boxes loudly on the side.*

KERRIE: Hear that?! It's empty. Every one of these is hollow. Life fled this place.

>*Beat.*

CLO: It was you. Wasn't it? The wax. In the engine.
KERRIE: ... You won't ever leave.
CLO: She needs me.
KERRIE: I'm tired, Clo. Tired of waiting around for an afterlife that's never gonna—
CLO: Six months. If you love me—
KERRIE: Twelve years!
CLO: ...
KERRIE: We got old, Clo. I can't wait anymore.
CLO: Okay ...
>If that's what you want.

KERRIE: It's the law.

>*Beat.*

>They're just bugs, Clo.
>Even the honey.
>Don't believe all that crap on the label.
>It's just bug spit.
>That's all.

>KERRIE *turns away to the hives. She upends a tin of petrol, soaking the empty boxes as* CLO *watches on. She sets the tin down. Pulls out a matchbox.*

CLO: Wait.

>KERRIE *sighs, ready for the next argument.*

>Let me.

>KERRIE *looks at her: 'Are you sure?'*

>Before I change my mind.

>KERRIE *passes the matchbox.*

Beat.

CLO *stands there, looking on a life's work. About to strike the match. Then—*

JOAN: Put that fucken thing down.

JOAN *enters, in her nightdress, with* MELISSA.

KERRIE: The bees are gone, Joan.
JOAN: Do this and they'll never come back.
KERRIE: This is a quarantine. Do what has to be done.
JOAN: Stay out of this!
KERRIE: There's things only a fire will cleanse.
JOAN: Clover, listen to your mother.
KERRIE: Clo, you strike that fucken match or you'll never be free.
JOAN: This is a matter for family!

DARYL *enters, without a bee suit, unnoticed.*

KERRIE: You call this a family?!
CLO: Stop it!
KERRIE: It's over.
JOAN: They'll come back!
KERRIE: And how are you gonna do that?
JOAN: [*to* MELISSA] Call them.

Beat.

MELISSA: What?
DARYL: Go on.
CLO: Daz?
JOAN: Get back inside.
DARYL: And miss this?!

Beat.

CLO: Well, go on.
    Call them.
    If you're really Harry's girl …

Beat.

MELISSA *closes her eyes. She might be concentrating. Hard.*

For a moment, nothing happens.

And then the air is electric. Perhaps the light seems to shift ... even for a moment.

DARYL: [*to* MELISSA] It was a trick.

And then it's gone.

JOAN: What are you doing?

DARYL: There's no magic. Dad didn't have any powers. He was just a good showman.

CLO: Daz, you should—

JOAN: Get back inside!

DARYL: But if you look past all the bullshit, it was simple. He was a charlatan. A fraud.

JOAN: I'm warning you.

MELISSA: Let him speak.

DARYL: You think he was the Wizard of Oz. He was just this horny little troll.

JOAN: That's enough!

Beat.

DARYL *swats the back of his neck.*

Beat. He looks at his hand.

DARYL: Oh.

CLO: Oh, fuck.

JOAN: Now you've done it.

KERRIE: I'll get the epipens.

KERRIE *exits.*

JOAN: Take him inside.

DARYL *sits down.*

DARYL: No, I think I'll stay here.

CLO: What are you doing?

DARYL: I just spoke to Hank. I think it went well ... He's still suing us, but I think he feels pretty bad.

JOAN: Get up.

CLO: Daz?

DARYL: It's so peaceful. Don't you think? Without all that noise.

CLO: We don't have much time.

DARYL: A bit chilly though. How about a fire?
JOAN: No.
DARYL: Then I'll come. When you've razed it to the ground.
CLO: …
DARYL: Well, come on. Chop-chop.
JOAN: You think you can blackmail me? Leave him.
CLO: No.
JOAN: You've made your point. Now get up.
DARYL: Nup.
JOAN: Get. Up.
DARYL: Burn it.
JOAN: You will not.

  KERRIE *enters with the epipens.*

KERRIE: Hold still.
DARYL: No.
CLO: Daz—
DARYL: First, you torch the fucking lot.
CLO: Okay fine.
JOAN: He's not allergic.

 Beat.

 That stops her.

CLO: What?

 Beat.

But he went to hospital.
He nearly died!
JOAN: That doesn't make him allergic.

 Beat.

CLO: No.

 Beat.

JOAN: How long have you known?
DARYL: You think there's no bees in Sydney?

 Beat.

CLO: You *knew*?!

DARYL: …
CLO: And you didn't tell me?
DARYL: …
CLO: You *knew* and you left me behind?
DARYL: I only found out later.
CLO: When?
DARYL: Clove—
CLO: When?
DARYL: It doesn't matter.
CLO: *When?!*
DARYL: I was twenty-one.

    Beat.

Even if I had have come back. You'd never have left his side.
CLO: And so you said nothing.
DARYL: …
CLO: [*with a laugh*] Her, I can understand. She's pathological. But you—
DARYL: You didn't want to know. Too busy worshipping at the altar of Harry.
CLO: At least he didn't lie to me!

    JOAN *laughs.*

I'm sorry?
JOAN: Nothing. It's done.
CLO: Just because he hated *you.*
JOAN: You think he cared?

    It used to break my heart. Watching you both fawn over him, desperate for attention. And him barely noticing you were there.
CLO: No. That's not true.
JOAN: It was pathetic.
CLO: Dad loved us.
JOAN: Harry never cared for anyone. It's the truth.
MELISSA: Then why'd he send the letters?
JOAN: Harry! Writing love notes like some moonstruck puppy. Can you imagine? Ha! No, I'm sorry, your father was cut from a different cloth.
MELISSA: But you told me—
JOAN: I told you he'd disappoint you.
MELISSA: I've got them. I've read them.

JOAN: And who do you think wrote them?

Beat.

I've been cleaning up after that man his whole life.

MELISSA: He said he loved me.

JOAN: Don't be ridiculous.

MELISSA: He did.

JOAN: Harry came to me like a dog with his tail between his legs who'd got another bitch pregnant and I took care of it because that's what I did. You're not special! You didn't come from anything special. She was just one of his whores. That's what you came from. A philanderer and a whore fiddling with each other out behind the stacks.

MELISSA: She told me he loved her.

JOAN: *He told them all!*

Beat.

Your father was a weak, pathetic man. He couldn't make the tough decisions. He was a summer king ruling the blue-sky days, but when the weather turned, then he was gutless. That's why he killed himself. Blew his head off and left the mess for me. And now you want to burn the only good thing he left behind. Well, I say no. I will not let you do this. Because the legacy matters. Not because of Harry. Fuck Harry. He didn't love you. Any of you. His heart wasn't big enough. I ran the farm. I built the business. And I held this family together. Not Harry. Me!

MELISSA strikes a match.

No!

CLO: Do it.

DARYL: Go on.

JOAN: Why are you doing this? To punish me? I did all of this for you. Put that match down!

MELISSA nods.

She drops the match.

Inferno.

SCENE TWENTY-ONE

Monday morning.

Smoke.

JOAN *is alone amongst the wreckage.*

Long beat. Then ...

The buzz of a single bee ...

Joined by another and another, then many—a steady thrum.

MELISSA *enters, overnight bag over her shoulder. She waits.*

JOAN: Where's Daryl?
MELISSA: Gone.
JOAN: And Clo?
MELISSA: Heading back to Sydney.
JOAN: We can fix this ... The two of us, together.
MELISSA: ...
JOAN: We'll need a few days, maybe a week to get the hives back in order.
MELISSA: I'm not staying.
JOAN: We'll need to hire new workers. I can have them ready by next week. A month at the latest.
MELISSA: I'm going.
JOAN: Then go.

> MELISSA *turns to exit, stops.*

MELISSA: Come with me?
JOAN: What will you do?
MELISSA: I don't know.
  Not this.
JOAN: Hmph.
MELISSA: You'll be alright?
JOAN: I'm not done yet.

> MELISSA *turns to go.*

MELISSA: You were right.
  The bees, they came back.
JOAN: Those aren't bees. They're flies.

Long beat.
But what else is there to say?
MELISSA *exits.*
The light slowly fades.

...

...

..

..

.

.

THE END

www.currency.com.au

Visit Currency Press' website now to:
- Buy your books online
- Browse through our full list of titles, from plays to screenplays, books on theatre, film and music, and more
- Choose a play for your school or amateur performance group by cast size and gender
- Obtain information about performance rights
- Find out about theatre productions and other performing arts news across Australia
- For students, read our study guides
- For teachers, access syllabus and other relevant information
- Sign up for our email newsletter

The performing arts publisher

www.ingramcontent.com/pod-product-compliance
Lightning Source LLC
Chambersburg PA
CBHW040256170426
43192CB00020B/2820